Praise for
Furious Pursuit

"These days, I'm more inclined to think God's anthropology—what God thinks about us—packs more heft and punch than our theology—what we think about God. Tim King and Frank Martin seem to think so too, and have written a book that draws us into the wideness and deepness of God's heart, showing us his fierce and tender affection even for sinners like me. King and Martin remind us that the good news has nothing to do with how good we are, only how loved."

—MARK BUCHANAN, author of *The Rest of God*
and *The Holy Wild*

"The message of this book can't be stated often enough: God loves us. Oh yes, he does. *Furious Pursuit* shows us that God's love is active and vibrant and on the chase for you and me. Others have said this before, but *Furious Pursuit* takes us one step further."

—SCOT MCKNIGHT, author of *The Jesus Creed*
and *Embracing Grace*

"If you're sick and tired of spiritual to-do lists, religious shoulds and oughts, and the self-hatred that comes from feeling unacceptable, you'll find in *Furious Pursuit* better news of a better story. Tim King and Frank Martin have given us powerful truth, well-told.

—BRIAN MCLAREN, pastor, author of *A New Kind of Christian* and *The Secret Message of Jesus*

FURIOUS PURSUIT

FURIOUS PURSUIT

WHY GOD WILL NEVER LET YOU GO

TIM KING
AND
FRANK MARTIN

WATERBROOK
PRESS

FURIOUS PURSUIT
PUBLISHED BY WATERBROOK PRESS
12265 Oracle Boulevard, Suite 200
Colorado Springs, Colorado 80921
A division of Random House Inc.

Details in some anecdotes and stories have been changed to protect the identities of the persons involved.

ISBN 1-4000-7149-6

Library of Congress Cataloging-in-Publication Data
King, Timothy R., 1959-
    Furious pursuit : why God will never let you go / Tim King and Frank Martin. — 1st ed.
        p. cm.
Includes bibliographical references (p.   ).
    ISBN 1-4000-7149-6
1. Providence and government of God. 2. Trust in God. I. Martin, Frank, 1958- II. Title.
    BT135.K56 2006
    248.4—dc22

                                    2006005744

Printed in the United States of America
2006—First Edition

10 9 8 7 6 5 4 3 2 1

To the Beloved, with eternal gratitude
for Gwynne and our three awesome children: Zac, Kelley, and Jason
—TIM

To Ruthie, David, and Kandilyn
—FRANK

CONTENTS

ACKNOWLEDGMENTS

An old adage says, "None of us is as smart as all of us." Certainly this is true regarding our present endeavor, and because of the following people, it is so much more than it would have been had Frank and I worked alone. I would like to thank Bruce Nygren and so many others on the WaterBrook staff for believing in this work from the start. Thanks to Ron Lee, an editor who invested his heart along with his skills in helping us frame this material in the best possible way. Thanks as well to Kevin Beck, John Trapp, Robert Costa, Doug King, Jay Gary, Les Lamoureux, and Jan O'Brien—my board of directors and constant associates—for providing excellent guidance, love, and critique.

Finally, to the Beloved: In the words of the psalmist, "Not to us, O LORD, not to us, but to your name give glory, for the sake of your steadfast love and your faithfulness."[1]

A NOTE BEFORE YOU BEGIN

Here are a few things you should know before you begin.

First, even though this book is a collaboration between two authors, we decided to write in the voice of one, using first-person singular. Constantly saying "We think this" or "We believe that" feels cumbersome, so we defaulted to the singular "I." The exceptions are the times when we tell a uniquely personal story. In those cases, we have indicated who is speaking in parentheses.

The second thing you need to know is that we took the liberty of changing names and certain identifying details wherever necessary. If you think you recognize someone from one of our stories, you're probably wrong!

Finally, the viewpoints and opinions in this book reflect beliefs we both share. The one rule we had going in is that no theological perspective or word of advice would find its way into the manuscript unless it was owned by both of us. What you will read in the chapters that follow represents our shared worldview about life and faith.

We hope our approach in this book will result in as much of a life-transforming experience for you as it has been for us.

—Tim and Frank

ONE

God's Heart Calling Yours

Stop Chasing God and Let Him Pursue You

Struggle with God is the essence of
relationship with God.
—James Emery White

Deep calls to deep
in the roar of your waterfalls;
all your waves and breakers
have swept over me....
"Why have you forgotten me?"
—Psalm 42:7,9

Not so long ago I (Frank) was on the phone with Andy, one of my dearest friends. We've known each other since grade school, and there's not an ounce of pretense between us, which is the thing I treasure most about our relationship.

I could tell that Andy was feeling down. He had been struggling through some tough life issues, so I tried to cheer him up by sharing some thoughts from a book I'd been reading about pursuing God with passion. The book talks about seeking God through spiritual disciplines such as prayer, fasting, and meditation. I could tell by Andy's silence that he wasn't buying into it. Finally he sighed and said, "You know what, Frank? I'm sick of chasing after God. I want God to chase me for a while!"

Even though these words came from the most brutally honest friend I have, I wasn't sure what to think. *Should he be saying such things—thinking such thoughts? Is there room in our relationship with God for such candor?*

Part of me wanted to remind Andy that God doesn't answer to us, that his thoughts are higher than ours, that if God feels distant to us there must be a reason for it, that it's not right to question God's ways, and that it's certainly not right to doubt him. But I didn't say any of that. In fact, what I did say surprised me.

"To be honest, Andy, I'm tired of chasing him too."

I still don't know exactly where that came from, but it was the most honest I'd been in a long, *long* time.

THE ZEN OF ZIGGY

There is a weariness that seeps into our spiritual lives. It doesn't come all at once, and thankfully it doesn't always stay long. But we've all tasted it, been frustrated by it, tried to pretend it doesn't matter. The weariness doesn't define our relationship with God, but it definitely messes with it. It confuses us and sometimes even indicts us.

Actually, *weariness* may not be the best word for what we experience from time to time. Let's call it a nagging sense that all is not right between God and us. We sense that our faith should be stronger, that our resolve should be more resolute, that our lives should be more in tune with God's will. And that we should be closer to God than we so often feel.

We speak of God's merciful love and our complete joy in having found it, yet deep in our souls we sense a strange divorce between our faith and our hearts. We can no longer deny the dark chasm that separates what we say about God from what we so often experience. There seems to be an identity crisis between the God we know and the God we *profess* to know. Like David, we cry out in our darkest hour, "Why, O LORD, do you reject me and hide your face from me?"[1] And still he seems silent and far away.

We follow hard after God, giving him the best we have to offer. And in response we get nothing more than this blasted suspicion that we're the ones doing all the work, that for some strange reason God isn't doing his part.

"I'm sick of chasing after God," Andy told me. Maybe he was speaking for a lot of us. Think about how many miles you've logged in the pursuit of God, often getting nothing back but silence and spiritual loneliness. Could this be the true source of your weariness, the reason your spirit feels drained? Maybe we're all just so dog-tired from chasing after God.

How many times have you sat in church as your minister outlined the steps to developing a deep and meaningful relationship with God? You'd love to have what he's promising, and based on the nods and smiles on every side, you assume it can't be that hard. You wonder if you're the only one in the sanctuary who hasn't quite gotten there, so you commit to trying harder. You promise yourself that you'll pray more, give more, study more, love more, and sin less. You'll chase God with everything you have, hoping it will cause him to draw near. Maybe then you'll know deep in your heart what it means to be a friend of God and not just a follower.

Weeks go by, and so does the busyness of life. Once again you find yourself in the same pew listening to the same words, and you're wearier than ever. You can't remember a time when you've been this confused and tired and apathetic. And the worst part is the feeling deep in your gut—the empty, agonizing feeling that perhaps you're the only one who has this problem. You're the only God chaser who can't seem to find him.

Ziggy sums up our angst in a nutshell. A single-panel cartoon depicted him standing in front of a huge shopping-mall map. The map had a small circle at the bottom left corner that read "You are here." At the top right corner, the farthest edge away, was a larger circle next to the words "Everyone else is over here."[2]

Can you relate?

You know it's not a question of faith. You love God, and in the deepest recesses of your heart, you know he loves you back. It's just that you don't always *feel* loved by God. And you rarely feel all that close to him. For a God who promised to be with us forever, to live within us and through us, he seems to excel at keeping his distance.

"Come near to God and he will come near to you,"[3] the Bible assures us. And we all know that God's Word can be trusted. But you have fought to draw near to God, struggled to find him and get close to him. And you still feel that he is distant and you are alone.

I (Frank) have a good friend named Barry who never seemed to have this problem. We were in a Bible-study group together, and every time we met, he had a quick smile and another exciting revelation from Scripture that he couldn't wait to share. It seemed he was always running across some stunning truth during his daily times of prayer and Bible reading. His joy seemed endless and fresh and vibrant—and exhausting.

I love Barry, but I couldn't for the life of me relate to him. Nothing about his experiences with God rang true. I was in a completely different circle—a circle of spiritual loneliness that I was sure I had all to myself.

Then one day after a morning golf game, Barry and I were having lunch in a quiet corner booth, and he began to share some of his struggles—intimate struggles he had never shared with anyone. Because of some bad career decisions, Barry found himself in a crushing financial squeeze, and the strain was becoming more than he could bear. He had prayed continually over his situation, pleading with God for help and direction—or at the very least, a little relief—but things never got better. In fact, the harder Barry prayed, the worse things appeared to get.

"I've given my whole life to serving God," Barry told me, "but when I need him most, he's nowhere to be found. It would be so easy for him to help me fix this problem, but he doesn't."

I searched my mind for some words of comfort, but none came. Finally Barry bowed his head, arched his shoulders, and whispered, "You know, Frank. I don't doubt that God is there, and I know he hears me. But sometimes I wonder if he even cares. I'm finding myself wondering if God is really good."

And this from Barry, the most plugged-in, spiritually devoted friend I have! If Barry can't find God, then what hope is there for the rest of us?

"Deep calls to deep in the roar of your waterfalls," David cried out in his suffering. "All your waves and breakers have swept over me.... 'Why have you forgotten me?' "[4]

Those words could have come right from Barry's lips, and there are days when they could just as easily come from yours or mine. You've been there, haven't you? You've cried out to God in your darkest hour for just a hint of help or clarity or comfort—and heard nothing but silence. You've prayed for direction in the wilderness only to find yourself more lost than ever. You've put your faith in an omnipresent God, even proclaimed him to your friends, and then wondered silently where he was when you needed him most.

But in your heart you know you're supposed to chase God—so you do. You continue to pursue him, to search for some kind of real and personal connection with your Creator, yet feeling all the while as if you're running in place. And the faster you run, the more exhausted you become. Eventually your heart grows weary, and you do the only thing you feel you can do: you succumb to spiritual numbness.

Don't you wish you could stop and let God chase you for a while?

God's Passionate Pursuit

What if I told you that's exactly what God does—that he not only chases you but never takes his eyes off you? What if I could prove that God has never gone a minute without thinking of you, wooing you, whispering in your ear, *I'm right here*? What if I could show you that God not only pursues you day by day, minute by minute, but he actually screams for your attention?

You don't have to chase God. All you have to do is awaken to his voice. He is never silent or out of reach or indifferent to what's going on in your life.

What if I went a step further and showed you that God's pursuit of you has absolutely nothing to do with your level of obedience and righteousness or your dedication to the spiritual disciplines?

Can you entertain the thought that God cannot *not* pursue you, that to leave you alone would run counter to his nature? He longs for an intimate relationship even more than you do. He is much more devoted to chasing you than you are to chasing him. And he has drawn near to you whether or not you ever choose to draw near to him.

If you could own the truth that God's relentless pursuit is more than just a comforting spiritual concept but is in fact the force that drives him more than any other, what would it mean to you? If you could believe that capturing you is God's all-consuming passion—all he thinks about from Adam to eternity—imagine how it would change your faith, your prayers, your reading of Scripture, and your view of God.

PURSUED BY LOVE

In M. Night Shyamalan's film *The Village* is a chilling scene in which Ivy Walker decides to travel through an unfamiliar forest to retrieve medicine for her ailing fiancé. Ivy is blind and the woods are thought to be inhabited by beasts—monsters referred to in the film only as "those we don't speak of."

Her father, Edward Walker, explains to the village elders why he would allow his blind daughter to go on such a perilous journey. They are angry with him because they know what dangers lurk in the woods.

"How could you have sent her?" asks one of the women elders. "She is blind."

Ivy's father bows his head and answers, "She is more capable than most in this village. And she is led by love. The world moves for love. It kneels before it in awe."[5]

Ivy Walker, though blind, is led by love.

Is there any more potent force than love? Is there anything in life that brings greater motivation, higher expectations, deeper introspections, better clarity? Is there an emotion that elicits more passion or brings out more fury?

"The world moves for love," says Edward Walker. "It kneels before it in awe."

When you are led by love, nothing is powerful enough to stop you. Nothing can discourage you from your quest.

And God is led by love.

More than that, God *is* love. It is his nature, his primary focus, his driving force. He is moved by love, provoked by love to press forward, to stay the course, to relentlessly pursue his beloved. Although he is grieved when we stray from him, he remains unfazed by our waywardness, undistracted by our inability to remain faithful. You and I are pursued by *Love*.

And the world moves for him. It kneels before him in awe.

This book is written for those who want desperately to believe that truth. It is for those who long to feel loved and wanted by God. It is for those who want to believe in the furious faithfulness of God yet struggle to see it. It is for those who want to trust deeply in the character of God.

This book is *not* for those who have it all together, who never question God or stumble as they try to follow him. If you don't struggle with sin, shame, grief, or loneliness, then by all means read something else. This book is for those of us who struggle with little else.

During that same scene in *The Village,* one of the town elders sums up his thoughts about the blind but persistent Ivy Walker journeying through the woods on her own. "Ivy is running toward hope," he says. "Let her run."[6]

We share Ivy's helplessness as she struggles through the wild and frightening woodlands, her hands stretching into the darkness as she feels her way through the thicket of trees and brush, fighting to make her way back home. She is stumbling, crawling, scratching her way forward.

This book is for those who feel like blind, helpless children stumbling through a dark and dangerous forest, falling, getting up, then falling again. Those who are fighting to make their way through the forest of faith, through the vast woodland of fear and doubt and confusion.

For all of us who have found ourselves running toward hope, welcome to a better Story of a much bigger God.

PART I

A ROMANCE TO BE EMBRACED

THE PASSION THAT DREW YOU

Isn't that the message of the Bible? The relentless
pursuit of God. God on the hunt. God in search.
—MAX LUCADO

For I will forgive their wickedness
and will remember their sins no more.
—HEBREWS 8:12

The most damaging lies we encounter in life tend to be the lies we tell
ourselves about ourselves. And the damage is multiplied because these
lies almost always go unchallenged.

Take the woman who has had more sex partners than friends, who has
two children but no husband, and who wants more than anything to know
God's love. The only thing that holds her back is a lie: she can't imagine
that he would accept her. *I'm worthless,* she tells herself. *Why would God*
want someone like me?

Or the man who once served as a church deacon until the bottle got the best of him—and lust got the rest of him. Now he can't meet the gaze of his friends, much less his former parishioners. *I had my chance with God, and I blew it.*

Or the pastor who speaks eloquently of God's love every week from the pulpit yet has never fully experienced it in his heart. He proclaims God's love while continually condemning himself with a lie: *I'm just a fake, and someday God is sure to expose me.*

These thoughts go completely unchallenged by what God tells us is true—and what he wants us to understand about his nature. And the hard truth is that transformation can't begin until we start to challenge these lies with a more complete understanding of God. Until we contrast what we tell ourselves to be true with what God says is true.

"Life is hard and then you die," we may tell ourselves. But God tells us, "Everything has *meaning*—everything you experience in life is either a product or by-product of my great pursuit."[1]

"My faith is so weak," we say. But God says, "It's not about your faith; it's about my faithfulness."[2]

"I'm just an unworthy sinner," we say. But God says, "You are not defined by what you do; you are defined by who pursues you."[3]

Whether or not we realize it, and whether or not we ever choose to accept it, you and I are caught up in the greatest and grandest Love Story of all time. It's the Story of a King who stepped down from his throne in order to win the heart of a fair maiden. It's beyond question "the greatest Story ever told," and it's a romance unlike anything you and I could ever imagine.

This is one Tale, one timeless Story, one eternal Romance that you don't want to miss.

TWO

GOD'S RELENTLESS PURSUIT

WHY HE CAN'T RESIST YOU

What comes into our minds when we think about
God is the most important thing about us.
—A.W. TOZER

If we are faithless,
he will remain faithful,
for he cannot disown himself.
—2 TIMOTHY 2:13

C an you remember a time when God was all you wanted or needed? Can you recall the last time your love for him was pure and uninhibited, undefiled by doubt?

Maybe it was when you first came to faith. Your heart longed to believe that there was more to life than living, loving, hurting, and then dying. And when you found God, you finally discovered the real meaning of life. The truth of the Cross brought you to your knees and you surrendered, giving yourself to a Lover and a Love Story unlike any you'd ever thought possible. You loved God with abandon, worshiped him from the depths of your spirit, honored him with your life and words. You couldn't imagine spending a moment outside his presence.

Or perhaps it was God's grace that captured your heart. You'd already accepted his salvation, yet it always felt conditional. And finally you were introduced to a forgiveness that is not only absolute but irrevocable. You'd been dancing *for* God, but then you found yourself dancing *with* him, and you never wanted the music to stop.

Most of us can recall a season when we were drawn inescapably into God's love—a time when our faith bordered on fanaticism. But then something happened. Life happened. Your love grew dim, and a slow deadness began to settle into your spirit. The struggles of living weighed you down, and God didn't always show up to help. So your faith gave way to doubt, trust turned to confusion, intimacy was replaced by abandonment. The music slowed, your feet grew weary, your Lover no longer looked so lovely.

I (Tim) have a vivid memory of sitting on a church pew at the age of twelve. A visiting missionary from Greece held me spellbound with tales of spiritual conquest and adventure on the mission field. He told of a great awakening of faith taking place overseas, and with all my heart I wanted to go back with him. I couldn't imagine anything better than spending my life leading people to Jesus, devoting every waking moment to his service. Even at a young age, I longed to do great things for God, to grow in wisdom, to give myself completely over to his will. I began praying incessantly for his guidance, his hand of blessing to make the deep desire of my heart a reality.

But somewhere between the puzzlement of puberty and the labor of life, I lost it. Not my faith, just the fire. I still loved God, but following him into an unknown land took a backseat to other interests. Theology, for one, proved more intriguing. So the flame that burned so hot and high at the age of twelve now gave off little more than a tepid glow.

When Flames Fizzle

Few people have a relationship with God that is free of this ebb and flow between all-consuming passion and apathy, between longing and suspicion. In fact, any encounter of the heart will eventually lead to apprehension and pain. But somehow we hope it will be different with God. We believe that he can be trusted, that he is completely loving and reliable. Yet at the moment of our deepest need, he is often nowhere to be found. When we most need him to be good, we imagine him to be indifferent or, at best, inconsistent. So we begin to pull away from him.

"We give ourselves to God," wrote James White, "and then struggle profoundly with the relationship. We are drawn inexorably in, and then find ourselves wanting to flee in fear.... We find that living with God is not easy."[1]

"Living with God is not easy"? That may well be the greatest understatement of all time. The truth is, living with God can be the most difficult thing many of us will ever do.

At the age of seventeen, I (Frank) found myself in a season of deep communion with God. I felt closer to him than I ever imagined a person could feel with another being, especially a divine one. It seemed that every waking moment was filled with thoughts of God's love, visions of his presence, and longings for an even deeper encounter with him.

One day I discovered a vacant storage room beneath a stairwell in our church. I began stopping there every day after school to pray. Soon I was setting my alarm clock to ring earlier in the morning so I could commune with God before school as well. My father had a key to the church, so I had the entire place to myself. Hour upon hour I whiled away my adolescence sitting in that small, dark room, praying, worshiping, meditating, seeking to draw nearer to God, and weeping at the power of his presence. My passion for God seemed endless and unshakable.

But time proved it to be neither. Within a few short years, I was running from the God I once adored, wondering what I had ever seen in him. I wrestled with deep feelings of abandonment and betrayal that went beyond apathy into the realm of contempt.

At twenty-two I wanted nothing to do with God. I wasn't sure I even believed that he existed. My spiritual journey didn't just come to a crossroads; it ended altogether. What began as a beautiful love affair ended in a bitter divorce. I resigned myself to a life of spiritual separation from God.

I lived, I worked, I chased girls. I remained morally upright, but only out of habit. In front of my friends and family, my religious facade was convincing, but my feelings toward God were dead. Nothing but memories remained between us. And the worst part of it was that God didn't seem to care too much either. He appeared to be as apathetic about the loss as I was. It was as if he'd never known my name.

The pain of our estrangement came to a head one night, almost out of nowhere. I was lying in bed in my small apartment, trying to slip my mind into neutral for a good night's sleep, but I couldn't do it. I couldn't put my thoughts at ease. I tossed and turned through the night, all the while wondering what was keeping me awake.

I was angry that I couldn't get to sleep. I had a big day ahead of me, work that had to be done, and I needed to be fresh. *Why can't I just go to sleep?*

And there in the quiet darkness of my own prison of isolation, I thought I heard God whisper. It was subtle yet real. I heard it in the depths of my spirit. *Why won't you talk to me?* he asked. *I've been waiting so long.*

My first instinct was to resist, to chalk it up to fatigue and anxiety. For a few short minutes it worked, until the voice came again. *What are you running from? Do you know how much I love you?*

Suddenly a well of sorrow and remorse burst from within my spirit. I wept harder than I thought possible. From the deepest part of my soul, the part I had ignored since separating from God, I cried out in pain and confusion, "God, I miss you so much. I'm so alone! I'm so tired of running."

With my head buried in my pillow, I cried through the night to the first glimpse of light, all the while pleading with God to take me back, to forgive me for straying so far from him, to help me rebuild the bridge that I had so callously burned, to make things between us the way they once had been.

God answered that prayer in the most powerful way. Not all at once, but little by little, day by day. He began rebuilding our relationship, restoring the trust, and renewing my shaken faith.

At the time it didn't occur to me what had really happened. God hadn't just *accepted* me back; he *wooed* me back. He initiated the romance, not me. All this time I was sure I'd had something to do with it.

THE LOVE OF A WILLING HEART

Danish philosopher Sören Kierkegaard once wrote about a king who loved a fair maiden. They were engaged to be married, but the king couldn't get over his uneasy feelings.

> Would she be happy in the life at his side? Would she be able to summon confidence enough never to remember...that he was king and she had been a humble maiden? For if this memory were to waken in her soul, and like a favored lover sometimes steal her thoughts away from the king, luring her reflections into the seclusion of a secret grief; or if this memory sometimes passed through her soul like the shadow of death over the grave: where would then be the glory of their love?[2]

The king longed to believe that the maiden could love him and that her love would be true and undefiled, but how could he know for sure? Should he bring her to the palace and cover her with silk and jewels? Or would this gain nothing more than a purchased heart?

Maybe he could go to her cottage and show her his glory and power, casting his huge shadow over her humble surroundings. *No,* he thought, *that would gain an overpowered heart.*

In the end the king knew that the only way he could truly win the maiden's love would be to descend to her level. So he decided to become a humble servant in order to gain the maiden's *willing* heart.

God could have decided to buy our love with the gift of a pain-free life and the promise of answering every prayer exactly as we desire. But he doesn't want our *purchased* hearts. He could conquer our stubborn will by displaying his might and supremacy and scaring us into submission. But that would gain him nothing more that our *overpowered* hearts.

God wants our *willing* hearts, so he chose to become a humble servant, to draw us into his love instead of buying us off or forcing us to love him.

Wouldn't you rather be drawn into a relationship than be pushed into one? Wouldn't you rather glide down the center aisle of your free will than stare down the barrel of a shotgun? Wouldn't you rather give your heart than have your heart taken?

God has wired us with the desire to be drawn into relationship. He created us to love us, but he gave us complete freedom to spurn his love. He created us as independent beings who control what we do with our hearts. And when we rejected his overtures toward us, he set in motion a plan to win us back—a plan that involved his becoming a humble servant.

Do you see how far the King was willing to go, how low he was willing to bend just to win your love and to woo your *willing* heart? Isn't this the God you long to embrace, the God you want desperately to trust in and to share a relationship with?

THE GOSPEL ACCORDING TO JERRY MAGUIRE

I (Frank) have almost no ability to recall details from movies, but one scene from long ago has stuck with me. In *Jerry Maguire,* Tom Cruise's character is standing in front of his angry, estranged wife, trying to express his feelings for her and win back her heart. From his blank expression, it's obvious he's at a total loss for words. The two stand face to face as he racks his brain, searching for the one thing he could say to alleviate her anger and show her how much he needs her. Finally, almost as a last-ditch effort, he says softly, awkwardly, "You complete me."[3]

Cue music. Wife's face softens and her eyes well with tears. She melts in his arms.

It is one of the corniest scenes ever put on film, yet many have a hard time watching it without breaking into tears. In fact, this on-screen moment provided the working definition of true love for a generation of movie fans. And is it any wonder? Don't we all want to hear someone say, "I need you," "I'm not whole without you," "Part of me is missing when you're not around"? Don't we all want to think that we complete the one who loves us most?

But Tom Cruise's character got it wrong. And so many of us got it wrong right along with him. Many have bought into a vision of love that is destined to fail, certain to crush any romantic relationship that is built on its shaky foundation.

What we've held up as the model for relational ecstasy is nothing less than a dysfunctional, codependent relationship on a collision course with disaster. It's a marriage destined to end in divorce. It is two incomplete people expecting the other to fill the void each of them feel inside. Any marriage counselor worth his salt will tell you how sad and damaging and unstable that kind of union is.

No relationship built on need can survive. It may start out with all the signs of true love and the highs and lows of a happy courtship. It may even look and sound like a perfect affair, but it can't last. Two incomplete beings can't combine to create a complete one.

Just ask any woman who feels trapped in a relationship. She may have thought she married for love, but somewhere along the way, she realized she married out of need. Now there are kids to raise, pets to feed, a mortgage to pay, and facades to maintain, but the love has long since faded from memory. She's stuck in a marriage she no longer wants. Her husband refuses to change, and she can't summon the energy to try anymore. But where else is she going to go? She needs someone in her life who needs her, and her need to be completed has trapped her in a loveless marriage.

A healthy marriage is based not on need but on two whole people deciding to form a meaningful relationship. Two people who are complete within themselves need nothing more than they already have. They choose to spend time with each other not because they need each other but because they long to be together. They come to the relationship not with *purchased* hearts or *overpowered* hearts but with *willing* hearts.

CREATED FOR DESIRE

I (Frank) was a senior in high school before I met my first self-declared atheist. Alan was a Canadian, and he and I worked together at a small bakery in Texas during the summer.

Alan said he was an atheist, but he was really an agnostic. He told me a number of times that he was willing to believe in God if God would just prove himself. "If he's real, why doesn't he show me?" Alan asked, though not always in a smug way.

I got the feeling that Alan wanted to believe, but he had no reason to. So I made it my personal goal to convince him of God's existence.

Alan and I worked side by side at the bakery eight hours a day, six days a week for nearly three months. It was the most agonizing summer of my life. Every discussion seemed to turn into a debate about the existence of God. I used every argument I could think of, but nothing would convince Alan. And his arguments would always end at the same place: "If God exists, why doesn't he just show himself? If he's as powerful as you say, then how hard could that be for him?" I never had an answer for him.

My prayers took on a different tone that summer. I found myself getting angry with God, asking him, "Why won't you show yourself to Alan?
Just send an angel one night to talk to him, to wake him from his sleep and
shake some sense into him. Prove to him you're there!"

All summer I pleaded with God to help me get through to Alan. But
God never once came to his own defense. Soon summer was over and Alan
went back to Canada, even more skeptical than before. His agnostic resolve
had grown even stronger over the summer, and my faith had grown weaker.

"Someday you're going to see how wrong you are," I told Alan on his
last day of work.

"All God has to do is prove it!" he said.

And Alan had a point. All God had to do was show himself. Just once!
Why wouldn't he do that?

We all know how easy it would be for God to prove himself, not just
to Alan but to every skeptic on the planet. He could eliminate all doubt in
one fell swoop, do away with any hint of skepticism, if he would just open
up the skies and reveal himself.

And he could do more than just convince us all to believe; he could
force us to obey him and to give him the honor he deserves. He could make
us fall on our knees and worship him. And yet he doesn't do any of those
things. God doesn't force us to believe in him. He created us to *desire* him.
He seeks the response of a *willing* heart.

THE BEAUTY OF DESIRE

On my desk is a photograph of my (Frank's) family. The four of us are
standing in a foot of snow in our front yard. Every time I glance at the
photo, I'm taken aback by the sight of my son, David. He's sixteen now, a

strapping young man. *When did he get so big? What happened to the little boy who used to climb on my shoulders?* I'm as proud as a father could possibly be, yet something in me longs for days gone by.

He was here in my office less than five minutes ago inviting me to go to Starbucks later this afternoon. Of course I said yes, though I should keep working.

David is an amazing kid. He's in love with life and crazy in love with Jesus, and today he's more than a son to me; he's my best buddy. There's nothing we'd rather do than spend time together. Yet there's a truth about our relationship that is hard for me to accept: David doesn't have to include me in his life. He has a car, he just got his first job, and he excels at school without even trying. He's incredibly bright, independent, and creative, and, yes, he's much better off with me in his life. But when you get right down to it, he really doesn't *need* me. He doesn't have to engage in a relationship with me. He's a complete person in his own right.

And yet he wants me to go to Starbucks with him! He desires to spend time with me. He longs for relationship with his father. And that thrills me beyond words.

Is there anything more beautiful, more exciting, more powerfully satisfying than when a completely whole and independent person chooses to be with you? When that already complete being loves you deeply just for who you are, with no ulterior motive, just a pure desire to spend time with you?

It is the greatest joy that life has to offer. And there is something very right, very satisfying, very *divine* about it.

CHOOSING THE HEART YOU GIVE

What would happen if you woke up tomorrow morning and flipped on the news only to learn that God had just announced that everyone on earth was saved? Or what if you went to church next Sunday, and God showed up to tell everyone that he had just done away with hell? Imagine that, from here on out, there was no longer any cause to worry about eternal judgment.

If you knew for certain that no one would end up in hell, would you still tell people about Jesus? Would you still have a compelling message to share? Would you have any motivation to try to reach those who don't know God?

If everyone on earth were saved, what could you say about God that might still appeal to people? Would you have enough of a relationship with God to talk passionately about his love and mercy? If you couldn't spare people the torments of hell, would you still want to make sure they knew how to enjoy a relationship with God?

How you answer those questions says everything about the nature of your relationship with God. So many of us were introduced to God through gripping tales of the terrible fate that awaits us in the afterlife unless we accept Jesus as our Savior. So we accepted Jesus as our Savior, and that truth came to define our relationship with God. What we call a "relationship with God" is little more than an eternal reprieve of the consequences of sin. We were confronted with the fires of hell and were told about God's power to keep us safe, so we came to God with an overpowered heart. And we stay with him out of fear of what might happen if we leave.

Or maybe that doesn't describe your experience. Perhaps you came to God through the door of love, through complete awe and wonder at the depth of his goodness. Your fascination with him was endless, your heart completely overwhelmed by his love and mercy.

But somewhere along the way, something happened. Someone told the fair maiden that her Bridegroom was no humble servant but a King, and she couldn't help but wonder just how rich and generous he was. So she started asking for presents and blessings and special privileges. She tested the breadth of his love with longer and longer wish lists.

It's a trap that's easy to fall into—and many have dived in headfirst. Entire religious movements are built around the premise of seeing how many good things God can do for you. And make no mistake: God can and does do very good things for you, but that's no basis for a real relationship. In fact, it's not a relationship; it's an arrangement. It's nothing more than a *purchased* heart. It's love with strings and conditions attached. And it's a far cry from the Story that God wants us to live in.

God's Story is the story of a King who came as a humble servant in search of a *willing* heart. It's the Story of a Creator who sets out in tireless pursuit of his creation. The Story of a Lover who went to war with all the forces of darkness in order to rescue his fair maiden and bring her home. God's Story is the Story of a Romance. A Romance to be embraced.

THREE

Leaving Your Story Behind

Trading Fear, Pain, and Loneliness for God's Unfailing Promise

I'm often surprised to find how my doubts
can mingle so freely with my faith.
—Mark Buchanan

I don't let go of my thoughts—
I meet them with understanding.
Then they let go of me.
—Byron Katie

For the purposes of our story, let's call him William.

I (Tim) met William during my first days as a minister. I was in my early thirties; he was in his midseventies. He had recently been diagnosed with an advanced case of emphysema and had very little time left.

William was a kind and gentle soul with a great sense of humor. I found myself wishing I had met him earlier, under different circumstances. He'd been a believer since childhood, had attended Bible college, and had even spent time as a Bible professor. His faith flowed easily from his lips, and in a matter of days, he'd be going home to be with God.

I was in my study the day I got the phone call informing me that William had been taken to the hospital. His disease had progressed more quickly than expected, and now he had just a few hours left.

I was completely unprepared for what I experienced when I stepped into William's hospital room. His family was huddled tightly together in the far corner, no one saying a word. In their faces I expected to see tears of sorrow, but instead I saw what can only be described as *fear*. And shock. As if someone had snatched a rug out from underneath them. I caught a glimpse of William's heart monitor, beeping and humming, the thin green line struggling to remain steady. The room was cramped with machines and lights and screens, all trained on the small bed in the center.

And there lay William, his hair wet and matted, his frail hands balled into tight fists, knuckles white with tension, his eyes frozen open. Jaws clenched shut and lips quivering, he looked like a wild, caged stallion fighting to break free from his bridle. I hardly recognized him. The peaceful, loving man I'd come to know had been ready to meet his Maker. But the man in this hospital bed was nothing like that.

"William, it's okay," I said, placing my hand on his shoulder. "Everything is going to be all right."

"No, it's not all right!" he screamed and pulled away from me. "You don't understand. It's not going to be all right!"

I reached for him once more, but again he pulled away. With tears pouring from his eyes he shouted, "You don't understand. You don't know what I've done!"

I sat dumbfounded as William began telling me why he was certain that his soul was lost forever. He described an incident that happened when he was seven years old. He had been sexually abused by a distant uncle, and this molestation had been eating at him, condemning him, haunting him with guilt and shame for nearly seventy years. And it wasn't even his sin! It was something that had been done *to* him.

I tried my best to console him, to explain that God was merciful and forgiving and that he had nothing to worry about. I tried to convince him that his soul was secure in God's mercy and grace. But all the while William continued to cry. He was in anguish over the fate of his soul.

That night William passed away fearing a condemnation that kept him still clinging hopelessly to earthly life. No words could console him.

TWISTING THE STORY OF GOD

No amount of seminary training can prepare you for that kind of encounter. No books or classes or conferences can teach you how to undo a lifetime of fear or reshape a damning life story in a single afternoon. Somehow "It'll be all right, William" wasn't enough.

Here was a man who had not only put his trust in God but who had lived for God and had taught others to do the same. How many thousands of sermons and Bible studies and seminars on God's nature had William sat through? How many Christians had he come into contact with? Why hadn't anyone been able to convince him of the grace, the mercy, the unconditional love and forgiveness of God? Why did William have to die without knowing the joy and comfort of God's furious faithfulness?

Standing in that hospital room and staring into William's terror-stricken eyes, I realized that God had given me a ringside seat to one of the great eternal battles between fear and love, and that day fear was kicking love's butt!

At that moment God spoke to me in a powerful way. I could all but hear him screaming into the depths of my soul: *Pay attention to this, Tim. I brought you here for a reason. You need to see this, to experience this, because William is just one of millions of my children who live in fear and worry and confusion. People have put their faith in me, yet they live in torment because they've never heard my Story the way it is supposed to be told.*

Somewhere in history, someone began twisting and watering down the Story of God. The "greatest Story ever told" has been perverted and transformed into the "scariest story ever told." Someone decided that the wrath of God is a more effective hammer for evangelism than the faithfulness of God, and since then it has been wielded so freely and wildly that we have lost sight of the real Story. The Story of God's faithfulness, even in the midst of our faith-*less*-ness, has been obscured. Love has been crowded out by fear.

In his first letter to the Corinthian church, the apostle Paul wrote that he "resolved to know nothing...except Jesus Christ and him crucified."[1] At some point in Paul's life, his message became completely focused. He homed in on the one truth that mattered more than all the others. This was the only thing he needed to know: that Christ's blood was enough. He knew and he wanted others to know there is "now *no condemnation* for those who are in Christ Jesus."[2] Adam's sin introduced fear and death and uncertainty into the world, but Jesus took it all away.

Standing in that cold hospital room with William and his family, I made that same resolution. I resolved that if I preached a thousand sermons and wrote a dozen books on God's nature, I would never veer from the simple but profound message of the Cross. Jesus' death for our sins proves the truth of God's faithfulness, even in the midst of our most horrific sin.

A STORY OF FEAR

"The sorrow of God lies in our fear of Him, our fear of life, and our fear of ourselves," wrote Brennan Manning.[3]

Ask most theologians what keeps men and women from God, and they'd probably say sin. But is that really the case? Isn't it fear that creates the greatest chasm? Fear of what God will do to punish us because of our sins?

Of all the stories people buy into regarding their relationship with God, perhaps none is quite as damaging or as common as the story of fear. We live in a state of dread, worry, and regret over our inability to remain faithful to God. We measure our relationship with God using a kind of "What have I done for him lately?" approach. We trust in God's goodness, but only as long as we've been obedient to him.

The story of fear has done more harm among Christians than any other false doctrine or errant theology we could conceive. It has immobilized more people—both believers and nonbelievers—and left more lives fractured and isolated than all other religious deceptions combined.

Think about what our fear says to God. It tells him, "You're not big enough. The Cross of Christ doesn't cast a wide enough shadow. Your promises can't be trusted."

We're afraid because we know we can't handle our sins, and deep inside we don't think God can either. We don't trust him to be good enough, loving enough, faithful enough, or forgiving enough to overlook the things we've done—not to mention the things we're yet to do.

Once, during a Sunday-morning Bible class, I asked a rhetorical question: "Which is the greater motivator—fear or love?"

"How would we know?" a lone voice shot back. "The church has never tried love."

This is the "sorrow of God" that Brennan Manning spoke of. The Story of God has been perverted into a man-made story of fear, and that breaks God's heart.

"It is one thing to feel loved by God when our life is together and all our support systems are in place," Manning wrote. "Then self-acceptance is relatively easy.... But what happens when life falls through the cracks? What happens when we sin and fail, when our dreams shatter, when our investments crash, when we are regarded with suspicion? What happens when we come face-to-face with the human condition?"[4]

Try to imagine what the story of fear says to the young woman who aborted her baby at sixteen only to realize later in life that she will be forced to live with overwhelming emotional pain. She keeps her secret out of fear and shame. Each year she suffers through the anniversary of her deed in silence, introspection, and regret. She knows God opposes abortion, and if she ever forgets, plenty of Christians stand ready to remind her. So where can she go with her remorse? She lives in a terminal state of fear. *How can God ever forgive me?*

And what about the man who struggles with an addiction to pornography? Years ago he nearly had the problem under control, but now he has a high-speed Internet connection. All the willpower he can muster isn't enough on the days when he's home alone with nothing to do. So he gives in, and later he wallows in guilt and shame. *I'm so weak and such a hypocrite. Why would God even listen to my prayers anymore?*

The story of fear invades all of our lives. And it grabs some of us by the throat and squeezes—never letting go.

And it's only one of the many damaging life stories that haunt us.

A STORY OF PAIN

Louie Anderson is a comedian who didn't have much to laugh about as a child. His father was an abusive, unpredictable alcoholic who made life miserable for the entire family. Anderson learned early that he could find comfort in food and developed a serious weight problem that has been with him ever since.

His comedy act is based on his painful childhood. He jokes about his drunken and angry father, his codependent mother, dysfunctional family dynamics, and his lifelong struggle with obesity. He tells story after story of a childhood mired in fear and rejection and violence, and even as you laugh hysterically, you find yourself wondering how he ever got through it. How could he have grown up in such an out-of-control atmosphere and learned to laugh about it?

Some years ago Anderson wrote a book titled *Dear Dad.* It's not so much a book as it is a compilation of letters he wrote to his dead father. In these letters he reveals his pain:

> I don't think you loved me. Maybe you did, but I never felt it....
> The really sick part is that somehow I have always blamed myself for
> your drinking problem. Maybe if he hadn't had so many children, I
> think. Maybe if I wasn't born at all. Maybe if I had done more to

help everyone. Maybe if there hadn't been so much pressure on you to pay so many bills. Maybe then you wouldn't have drank.

Maybe not.

I don't know. I'd like to know, but I don't know how to find out.[5]

How many lives are defined by pain and confusion? How many people find their relationship with God marked by feelings of anger and bitterness?

I (Frank) have a friend whose son was diagnosed with a muscle disease during his teenage years. This young man lives in constant pain and frustration, unable to even tie his shoelaces properly. He has resented God ever since his diagnosis, swearing he will never forgive God for allowing this tragedy. He calls his parents' faith a fairy tale and offers his condition as definitive proof that if God does exist, he's at the very least indifferent and at the very most mean and vengeful. This young man lives in a story of pain, and that story is the only one that seems to bring any sense to what he's going through.

Pain can define a life. "We never really say that it hurts, really hurts," wrote Louie Anderson, "and so we spend the rest of our lives trying to make up for it, holding on tightly to things that we should really let go of."[6]

A story of pain. We all deal with it to some degree. We try to explain it away, try to make some sense of it, and yet the answers elude us. The reasons for pain and suffering seem as intangible as God himself. So we spend our lives "holding on tightly to things that we should really let go of."

"We need a story larger than the story of our pain...," observed James Emery White, "a story that places God in the midst of our suffering so that love would win the day."[7]

But where are we going to find such a grand Story?

A STORY OF LONELINESS

"I cried out to God for help; I cried out to God to hear me," wrote the psalmist. "When I was in distress, I sought the Lord; at night I stretched out untiring hands and my soul refused to be comforted. I remembered you, O God, and I groaned; I mused, and my spirit grew faint."[8]

There is yet another story that runs through each of our lives. It seeps in during moments of doubt or confusion or helplessness. For some of us, this story is a hurdle in our relationship with God; for others it is an immovable barrier.

It is the story of loneliness, a tale of distress and abandonment. It's the story of feeling deserted by God in our darkest hour, a story of oppression and bondage, of being vulnerable to things we should be able to overcome.

Dan Allender writes of a time when he woke up in a hotel room in a cold sweat, his body racked with pain. He was only forty at the time, yet he was riddled with the early signs of arthritis. He couldn't sleep, could barely even move, so he took out his journal and began to write.

> It is early in the morning and my joints ache. The bed is damp from fear as I look into my future....
>
> The terror that has descended seems magnified in the darkness of a foreign bed.... My hands ache, and I cannot grip the sheets to move to a new position without pain....
>
> I feel loneliness, then fury. How can this happen? My fury glides into envy. Then I round the corner into stark, naked terror. All in the span of minutes, my emotions race like a wind through an open window, blowing every unfastened paper into a chaotic debris.

What do you want from me, God? Will you gain greater glory through my crippling? I will not survive, unless I know something more about Your purpose. What must I comprehend to understand You?[9]

For some of us, the story of loneliness is debilitating, an inconceivable helplessness, a cry from the deepest chasm of our soul to a God who seems to be nowhere near. It is a feeling of being completely alone in our agony.

In his book *Touching the Shadows,* Bruce Nygren told the story of his wife's struggle with terminal cancer and their journey toward coming to terms with the disease that eventually took her life. Nygren wrote candidly about his anger and resentment toward God, and his struggle with loneliness:

My aching soul longed to weep.... In the dark I talked to God, begging for a reprieve: "This is Your deal; just help me to fit in with Your plans!" I would plead.... But too often I felt nothing.[10]

How often have you and I felt so completely isolated and forgotten when we most needed God's help? The story of loneliness is perhaps the most common story of all.

"I remembered my songs in the night," wrote the psalmist. "My heart mused and my spirit inquired: 'Will the Lord reject forever? Will he never show his favor again? Has his unfailing love vanished forever? Has his promise failed for all time? Has God forgotten to be merciful?'"[11]

In one way or another, the story of loneliness is the story of us all. We've all felt abandoned at our time of greatest need. Haven't we all wondered along with the psalmist if God has somehow forgotten to be merciful?

The stories of fear, pain, and loneliness are but three types of the many stories we hang on to. These stories fracture our faith and prevent us from developing a full relationship with God. They are stories we tell ourselves about ourselves, stories we tell ourselves about God and his relationship to us, stories we hang on to yet refuse to challenge. They are lies, false stories we should let go of.

If only we knew how.

The Story of God

Four thousand years ago, God made a covenant with Abram, whose name was later changed to Abraham. Actually, God made a covenant *for* Abram, since Abram had little to do with it. It happened just fifteen chapters into the book of Genesis.

In this covenant God promised to use Abram to form a mighty nation and to give Abram too many descendants to count. Abram would be the father of a nation God would use to bless all the nations of the earth. This was not a covenant primarily for Abram; it was a covenant for all humanity. To establish the covenant and to seal his promise, God "cut covenant" with Abram.

In Abram's day, cutting covenant was a ritual in which covenantal partners would hew an animal in two and place the severed halves on each side of a pathway. The partners of the covenant would then walk between the bloody halves of the carcass. The pledge they were making was a solemn twofold promise. Not only did they pledge to walk faithfully together within the boundaries of their promise, but they also pledged to suffer the same fate as the severed animal if they broke the covenant.

When cutting covenant, both partners would walk the pathway together, side by side. Except this time. As always, the pathway had been marked with blood, and the halves of the carcass had been laid out along the edges. Everything was ready except for one critical thing: God had put Abram to sleep. And as Abram slumbered, God himself walked the pathway—alone.[12]

The Hebrews writer tells us, "Since there was no one greater for [God] to swear by, he swore by himself."[13] This was one covenant that would depend on God alone, and he alone would pay the penalty if the covenant were somehow broken.

God was so intent on seeing the promise fulfilled that he took no chances. He knew that his covenantal partner was fickle and skittish. When left to his own devices, Abram was driven by fear and shortsightedness, willing to pass off his wife as his sister or sire a son by his wife's servant. Abram's faith was like our faith—weak, undependable, and uncertain.

God knew that a covenant of this magnitude—an *eternal* covenant—had to be established on something much greater than human resolve. It required a level of faithfulness that only an all-powerful, all-loving, ever-faithful God could offer. So he walked alone between the halves of a bloody carcass. He pledged to carry the covenant on his own shoulders.

Don't miss the magnitude of this act and the power of the Story of God. God was so convinced of his ability to remain faithful and so determined in his plan to restore us to himself that he was willing to lay everything on the line. When God walked between the severed animal pieces, he was saying to us, "This has never been about *your* faithfulness; it's about my faithfulness. It's not about your strength, your ability to remain in covenant with me. It's about my strength, my ability, my love, my resolve to save you. I pledge to fight for you, to stay in relationship with you, to walk with you no matter what, from now until eternity."

God knew that our faithfulness is like the morning dew, fragile and short-lived. He knew we would never be able to keep the covenant, so he pledged to keep it for us. He took the responsibility off our shoulders and put it on his own. When he cut covenant with Abram, he was actually cutting covenant with himself to make absolutely certain that the covenant would go unbroken.

He replaced our story with his Story, our faith-*less*-ness with his faithfulness.

This is the furious pursuit of God in all its glory, passion, and power. This is the Story of God that needs to replace our smaller stories of fear, pain, and loneliness.

LETTING GO OF THE SMALLER STORY

What if William, while lying on his deathbed, could have replaced his story of fear with God's Story? What if all the Louie Andersons of the world could learn to let go of their stories of pain, the lies that disfigure their lives? What if they could instead tap into God's Story?

What if we could take our stories of loneliness and rejection and realize once and for all that we've been telling ourselves a lie? What if we could adopt God's Story instead and embrace the truth that we are never alone, never distant from God?

Of all the life stories we live, only one is based in reality. Only one brings meaning to everything that happens to us. Only one has the ability to free us from the lies, the "things that we should really let go of."

Or maybe we should say that only one Story can get us to a point where our small, destructive, life-denying stories finally let go of us.

FOUR

FINALLY, YOU ARE UNDERSTOOD

HOW GOD'S COMPLETE KNOWLEDGE
OF YOU SETS YOU FREE

To be unknown of God is altogether
too much privacy.
—THOMAS MERTON

O LORD, you have searched me and known me....
You understand my thought from afar.
—PSALM 139:1–2, NASB

S itting on my (Tim's) shelf is a small but daring book by Natalie Goldberg on the craft of writing. It is titled *Writing Down the Bones,* and it's
easily the most insightful book on the subject that I've read. It encourages
readers to journal their thoughts—not just the big ones, but every thought,
every idea or notion that comes to mind. Goldberg has done this for many
years.

Each morning she writes down whatever thoughts come to mind—her
greatest fears and anxieties; her desires and disappointments; her highs,
lows, and in-betweens; her feelings on love and sex and romance, on success and failure, on humanity, on God. She shares the most intimate details
of her life with her journal. No thought or emotion is safe from exposure.
It is a daily exercise in gut-level honesty that Goldberg believes to be a critical practice for anyone who is serious about the art of writing.

It's a remarkable idea but not nearly as easy as it sounds. I have tried to
practice this discipline over the last several months. I've attempted to write
down every feeling and emotion, every thought—stupid, sinful, or otherwise—every fear and anxiety. I quickly learned that in order to write such
things down, I first have to be willing to acknowledge them on a conscious
level. Then I have to summon the strength to let the words flow through
my pen. It's a frightening exercise in transparency that doesn't come naturally to any of us. And once done, you're faced with the hardest part of all:
finding a safe place to hide your journal!

Goldberg calls the practice of daily journaling "freeing," but that's not
the first emotion you experience. The first thing you experience is embar-
rassment, followed by shame. And shame is followed by the fear that someone might find out who you really are. Some things are better kept hidden,
at least that's what I thought until Goldberg told an unbelievable story.

She was visiting with an upstairs neighbor one day and mentioned that she was planning on throwing out some of her journals. Her neighbor, who also happened to be a friend, encouraged her not to get rid of them, so instead, Goldberg did the unthinkable. She gave the journals to her friend!

A few days later, Goldberg's friend dropped by to see her and remarked, "I've been reading your notebooks all weekend. They are so intimate; so scared, insecure for pages.… It feels so funny."[1] The woman couldn't believe that Goldberg would be so open and vulnerable.

Incredible! Who among us would let someone else dive so deeply into the hidden corners of our lives? Would any of us let someone know us so intimately? Yet Goldberg did just that! And it wasn't as if the neighbor had been a lifelong friend.

"I don't care that she sees how I really am," Goldberg said. "I want someone to know me. We walk through so many myths of each other and ourselves; we are so thankful when someone sees us for who we are and accepts us."[2]

Imagine that all your thoughts over the course of one month were laid bare so that anyone who wanted to could see them. Every mean and bitter notion, every judgmental impulse, every angry urge, every sin (whether real or imagined), every wicked and immoral reflection. Most of us would never let this happen. And if somehow it did, we'd want to curl up and die. No one wants to be known that deeply.

Yet God knows each of us that deeply. God, the One in front of whom you will one day stand, knows you deeper even than you know yourself. He knows the most intimate and embarrassing details of your life.

And you know that he knows.

Doesn't that explain why so many of us are afraid of God and spend so much time worrying about what he thinks of us? Isn't that why we're tied up in knots about our relationship with him and our prayer lives are consumed with thoughts of remorse and shame?

Isn't that why we struggle to accept the fact—no, not to accept it, but to *internalize* the fact—that God loves us wholly and unconditionally? That he embraces us just as we are—thoughts, blemishes, doubts, and all?

A BEAUTIFUL MIND

Friedrich Nietzsche was one of the greatest minds of the nineteenth century, but you and I probably know him best as one of history's most zealous atheists. Much of his life was dedicated to disproving the existence of God. But what brought him to that point?

Nietzsche's father died when Nietzsche was only four, and he was raised by his mother and grandmother, two aunts, and a sister, all of whom were Bible-thumping Christian fundamentalists. They constantly chastised him and taught him about a god of rules and regulations, a god of wrath and anger and iron-fisted judgment. As he grew up, Nietzsche came to hate and reject this god. He used his brilliant intellect to try to expel any hint of Christian thought from the world. He wrote and lectured on the utter foolishness of believing in a higher power and threw his energy into trying to banish the god his family had taught him about.

Here's the irony: You and I should reject that same god. And like Nietzsche, we should dedicate our lives to helping others do the same. Because that god is not the living God!

When you see what drove Friedrich Nietzsche to disavow his mother's faith, you not only understand him, but you have to applaud him. He instinctively realized that such a god was not worth following—and certainly not worth loving. He renounced belief in a schizophrenic, wrath-hungry god because he knew that such a god could not exist.

Sadly, not everyone arrives at the same conclusion. Too many of us have bought into the faith we've been fed. Too many have lived our lives believing in a dualistic god, a god who loves us when we're good, rejects us when we're bad, and keeps a detailed record of both.

When a vengeful god knows your every thought and sin, your every fear and failure, you have absolutely no hope of gaining his approval. In the words of Brennan Manning, "The God of the legalistic Christian…is often unpredictable, erratic, and capable of all manner of prejudices.… The legalists can never live up to the expectations they project on God."[3]

Friedrich Nietzsche's family never told him the true Story of God, and eventually he grew to despise God. Most of us only grow to fear him.

LONGING TO BE UNDERSTOOD

Whether or not we ever choose to accept it, God loves us wholly and unconditionally in spite of our penchant for sin and rebellion and in spite of our faithless tendencies. His love is unlike anything we could possibly fathom on our own.

The great Baptist minister Will Campbell summed it up succinctly: "We're all bastards, but God loves us anyway."[4]

One of the hardest truths any of us will ever grasp is that God is completely enamored with us, absolutely smitten, in love with us unconditionally with all his heart and soul! He loves us regardless of anything we've done, thought, said, or felt. Is it possible to convince ourselves that the God who knows our every flaw could love us still?

King David wrestled with this truth. We see it in the self-effacing tone of so many of his psalms. He wrote openly of his depravity in the face of God's unshakable goodness and mercy, and yet somehow he was able to comprehend that God still loved him. He found a way to rest in the love and faithfulness of God, and in Psalm 139 he gives us a glimpse of why that was possible: "O LORD, You have searched me and known me.... You *understand* my thought from afar."[5]

David realized that God knew his every thought and action yet loved him deeply because he also *understood* what prompted those thoughts and actions. God understood David's pain, the past, and the pressure that drove David to do things he otherwise might not have done. God saw David's sin, but more than that, he saw the struggles and the humanity behind that sin.

Isn't that the depth of understanding we all long for? To be known not for what we do but for who we are in spite of our shortcomings? God knows we are riddled with sin and doubts and failures, but he also knows that we long to do better, to be better.

Last year my wife and I (Frank) helped lead a small group of middle schoolers in a weekly Bible study. One of the kids, a rowdy boy named Stephen, was constantly fighting to be the center of attention. He never took the study seriously, never worked on his memory verses, and never made comments that were on topic. Stephen annoyed the other kids, and as hard as we tried to mentor him, he kept pushing us away.

One night at dinner Stephen's name came up in conversation. My daughter Kandilyn told us how sorry she felt for him.

"Why?" we asked.

"You wouldn't believe how his mother treats him. She screams at him for no reason, and she does it in front of everyone. She insults him and puts him down right in front of his friends."

Our son, David, had witnessed this same verbal abuse on a number of occasions. "All the kids know about it," said Kandilyn. "That's why I feel so sorry for him."

Suddenly I felt sorry for Stephen too. I had no idea what he had been going through, and now I began to understand why he fought for attention.

He was struggling hard to be liked. When I began to understand him, it made all the difference in how I saw him and thought about him.

Stephen didn't know how to express his longing, but what he sought from the Bible-study group was someone who would understand him. In the end, that's what we all want most from any relationship. We don't want just to be known; we want to be *understood.*

UNDERSTANDING RAY

If anyone needed to be understood, Ray did.

Ray was a deacon in the church I (Tim) pastored many years ago. He was a good-hearted man, but he wasn't the sharpest pencil in the box. In many ways that's what we loved most about him. He was simple and unpretentious and unaffected. And he was willing to do anything we needed. The problem was, there wasn't much Ray could do very well.

My co-pastor and spiritual mentor at the time was Kurt Picker, and the two of us put our heads together to find something Ray could do. We came up with a great solution. Ray could be the deacon in charge of the auditorium setup.

Six months earlier our congregation had moved into a newly built gymnasium that doubled as a sanctuary on Sunday mornings. It was phase one of our long-term building plan. The church had started in a living room just a few years earlier and had grown to more than five hundred members, so you can imagine how excited we were to finally have a place of our own.

One day Kurt and I set up the auditorium just the way we wanted it, then we brought Ray in to show him. We said, "Ray, we want you to draw a schematic of the building. Do you know what a schematic is?"

Ray nodded his head.

"Okay, draw a schematic of the auditorium just the way we have it set up so you can set it up this way every week. We want you to be in charge of that. Do you think you can do that?"

"Yeah, I can do that," he said.

"If you have any questions, don't be afraid to ask, because this is a critical job," we told him.

Ray seemed to have a good handle on things, so we handed him the keys and turned the job over to him.

Nothing could have prepared us for the shock we felt as we stepped into the auditorium the following Sunday morning. Kurt, Ray, and I stood side by side. Ray was grinning from ear to ear; Kurt and I were stunned.

The auditorium was set up exactly as we had asked, all five hundred chairs lined up perfectly, even the ones behind the speaker's platform. But on the floor, around the end of every leg of every chair, a small square had been drawn. Ray had taken permanent markers and traced around the base of two thousand chair legs! Little red and blue squares covered the gymnasium, drawn with indelible ink on our brand-new indoor-outdoor carpet.

As I stood looking at Ray, who was still beaming with pride, everything within me wanted to scream, "Ray, what were you thinking? How could you possibly have thought this is what we wanted?"

But before I had a chance to say anything, Ray's grin started to disappear. You could almost see the wheels turning in his brain as he started making the connection between what he'd done and what he was supposed to do. He cocked his head slightly to one side as his eyes scanned the room. His mouth dropped open slightly. He didn't say a word, but I swear I could hear what was going through his mind. *Ray, what were you thinking?*

Nobody, not even Ray, understood what could possibly have been going through his mind as he crawled on the floor drawing tiny squares around every chair leg in the auditorium. Who would do that?

OUR GREATEST MYSTERY

We've all had moments like that, moments when we look back on something we did or said—something stupid or evil or both, something completely out of character—and thought, *What was I thinking?* We fall and stumble into sin, we do things we know in our hearts we shouldn't do, and later we hang our heads in shame, beating ourselves up and wondering, *What would make me do such a thing?*

An alcoholic goes to an office Christmas party after ten months of painstaking sobriety and, in a moment of weakness, reaches for a martini as the liquor cart passes by. Two weeks later he's back in rehab.

A young mom loses her temper and screams at her kids, then later she lies in bed crying and wondering what they must think of her.

A fifteen-year-old girl with her entire life ahead of her sits alone in the bathroom while her parents are out, fighting back tears as she waits to check the color of the home pregnancy test.

Each is baffled by the same mind-numbing question: *What was I thinking?*

We're all dumbfounded by our tendency to be so inconsistent and untrue to the better nature we know God has placed within us. There are times when all we can do is take a deep breath, throw up our hands, and ask, "What made me do that?"

As oversimplified as it may sound, the only answer we'll ever be able to give is "We may never understand." But we don't necessarily need to understand. All we need to know is this: *God understands.*

We talk a lot about the mystery of God, but is God really the greatest

50

mystery we grapple with? Hasn't he revealed to us everything we need to know about him? Hasn't he already told us his plan for humanity, his desire to be in relationship with us, and how he restored us to himself through the Cross? Granted, many things about God will remain a mystery, but he will not keep from us the things that are critical to our lives. He has revealed all we need to know about his grace and glory and purpose.

God's nature is not the greatest mystery we face. The greatest mystery we face is *our own* nature—our struggle with our humanity, our inconsistencies, and our insecurities. The most perplexing mystery is not understanding who God is but understanding why we do the things we do.

But we are not a mystery to God. We do not confuse him. He understands us because he created us. He knows our frailties and struggles, and he knows what we go through in our efforts to overcome them. He understands the humanity that drives us to do things we know are destructive— to fall off the wagon, to scream at our kids, to give in during a moment of passion, to draw two thousand squares all over a gymnasium floor—and then later slap our foreheads and say, "What was I thinking?"

God understands! And that is a very, *very* good thing!

You and I can spend a lifetime trying to figure ourselves out. We can go to counselor after counselor or earn a doctorate in psychology and never come to terms with the mystery of our failures and internal conflicts. We may discover bits of information that shed some light on our humanity, and we may even develop skills and tools to help us navigate through life a little better. But we will always be confused by our thoughts and actions. Our nature will forever be the source of our greatest frustration.

Still, our flaws and frailties are not what we need to understand. What we most need to grasp is that *God understands*. He wants us to believe, to *truly* believe, that in spite of our unlovable, incompetent, inconsistent, sinful selves, he loves us unconditionally. His nature doesn't allow anything less.

GRASPING THE SIGNIFICANCE

Jack London's short story "To Build a Fire" was written in 1902 and has since become an American classic—for good reason. The story tells about a rookie prospector in the Yukon who sets out on a long journey with his dog as his only companion. He ignores the advice of a more experienced man and trudges into the bitter cold, convinced that he can beat the elements. When night comes and the temperature drops, he realizes he's made a mistake, but it's too late. All he can do is try to survive the night.

It's a powerful story of a man trying desperately to stay alive in brutal conditions and living with the consequences of his poor choices. In the end he doesn't make it.

London later wrote this about the young prospector:

The trouble with him was that he was without imagination. He
was quick and alert in the things of life, but only in the things, and
not in the significance. Fifty degrees below zero meant eighty-odd
degrees of frost. Such fact impressed him as being cold and uncomfortable, and that was all.[6]

How often are you "alert in the things of life, but only in the things, and not in the significance"? How often do you hear a truth about God and even come to believe it, yet never quite connect the importance of it to your life? How often do you see the things of the Story of God, but only the things, not the significance?

You can't move forward in your faith unless you first realize the significance of being understood by God. God is the only One who knows everything about you, including your deepest secrets and your darkest failures.

That's cause not for alarm but for deep joy, because God understands what is behind everything in your life, both the good and the bad. The God in front of whom you will one day stand is the same God who fully understands you. And he is the same God who *defends* you. Your loving and understanding Creator is your only Defender, and he is always faithful.[7] Your lack of faith and failure to remain faithful can never diminish God's love for you.

You must internalize this truth, let it soak into your heart and soul. You need to weigh the effect this truth has on every aspect of your relationship with God. Study it, meditate on it, weep over it. You can't just look at this truth and say, "Isn't that cool? God understands me." It's not that kind of truth. This reality, this aspect of God, changes everything!

God sees into the most hidden corners of your heart and yet pursues you relentlessly in spite of everything because he *understands* you. Think about what that says about God, and what it says about you.

If all the Love in the universe is fully engaged in pursuing you, in courting you and winning your heart, if this is the end result of God's divine *understanding,* then what makes you think there is any room left in your life for fear and worry and doubt? What could make you think the small stories of your sin could somehow push God away? That your moments of weakness could ever diminish the power of God's passion for you or that your unfaithfulness could possibly overshadow his furious pursuit of you?

Do we really think our small stories are that powerful?

When you grasp the significance of being understood by God, you realize perhaps for the first time that the Story is not about you. The Story of God isn't about your sin; it's about God's love. It isn't about your faith; it's about God's faithfulness. It isn't about what you need to do to catch God; it's about what he has already done to captivate you.

Whether or not you like it, whether or not you ever fully grasp the concept, you are playing a part in history's greatest and grandest Love Story. And although the Story is not about you, it has everything to do with you.

FIVE

GOD'S LARGER STORY OF LOVE

TRADE THE LAW FOR THE LAW OF LOVE

[God] will use you to accomplish great things on
the condition that you believe much more in his
love than in your own weakness.
—MOTHER TERESA

You live by shedding.
—ROBERT FROST

Have you ever wondered why some literature is called *classic* literature? Why does one novel or short story make the cut while most go unnoticed?

The short answer is that there really are no short answers to these questions. But I'll attempt one anyway. What makes a story a classic isn't necessarily that it appeals to the masses, but that it *speaks* to the masses. A book or story achieves classic status when it speaks to the human condition during a specific time in history.

Every now and then a story comes along that communicates to an entire generation. It sums up our thoughts and emotions and describes our world more powerfully than we can. The story strikes a collective nerve, and just about everyone winces from the pain. Eventually everyone begins to recognize the work as a classic, and the reputation sticks.

Take Ernest Hemingway. His first novel, *The Sun Also Rises,* won the Nobel Prize in Literature in 1954 and has long been considered one of the greatest literary works of the past century. It has been praised as a timeless tale that speaks to all generations. But have you ever read it?

The Sun Also Rises, set in the bars and cafés of Paris during the 1920s, tells about a group of young Americans who are trying to enjoy life after the First World War. Most of the characters are weak and deeply conflicted. They are drunk through much of the story, and they struggle with self-doubt and bouts of moral and ethical failure. The narrator and leading character is Jake Barnes, an impotent war hero who pursues a married woman and is the most "together" person in the story. The novel reeks of shallow and immoral characters struggling to make their way through the confusion of life.[1]

One critic called Hemingway the "prophet of a lost generation."[2]

Another described Hemingway's characters as people who had "the courage to endure rather than the courage to do."[3] For all their trying and whining and fighting, they could never quite rise above their circumstances. They were conflicted and deeply flawed, living in a hard, unforgiving world. And for all their trying, the best they could hope for was simply to endure.

And look at Willy Loman, the troubled and misguided lead character in Arthur Miller's *Death of a Salesman*. Loman is a salesman who can't sell, a father who can't relate to his kids, a husband who's unfaithful to his wife, an aging dreamer who fails at everything he tries. He's a sad and lonely man living in a world that completely overtakes him. But when the play opened in 1949, audiences lined the block night after night to see it. Soon afterward, *Death of a Salesman* won a Pulitzer Prize for Drama.

Or think about the most studied poem of the twentieth century: "The Waste Land" by T. S. Eliot. He won the Nobel Prize in Literature in 1948 for his ability to capture the soul of a generation, yet his works are filled with darkness and despair. "The Waste Land" is a fractured, disconnected poem about desolation and death. And it, too, achieved the rank of classic literature.

What does all this say about the state of Western literature? You'll have to ask someone who studies such things. I'm more interested in what it says about the human condition.

Once when he was asked about his writings, Hemingway explained that he simply wrote what he saw and felt in the best and simplest way possible. Like most great writers, he wrote what he knew best. He captured on paper the deepest fears and yearnings of his heart, and when others read what he had written, his words struck a nerve. The same is true for Eliot and Miller and many, many other classic writers. They simply wrote from their gut, and people responded.

THE COURAGE TO ENDURE

"The courage to endure rather than the courage to do." Does that describe anyone you know? It describes Gaylan pretty well.

"I never wanted a family," Gaylan told me (Frank) once. "I have enough trouble just taking care of myself."

Gaylan was working for me, and he'd just left his wife and kids for the second time since I'd known him. Over coffee he told me, "I'm just not wired to be a father. I've been trying for years, and it just doesn't work. I love my wife and kids; I just think they're better off without me. I've got too much baggage, and it's not fair to lay it on them. I just want to get away and be by myself for a while. I'm not happy and she's not happy, so what's the point of trying to stay together?"

Nothing I said could convince Gaylan otherwise. He left, I left, and we never saw each other again.

When I first met Rod, he spent much of the afternoon telling me about his previous career as the CEO of a multimillion-dollar contracting firm. The company employed more than six hundred people, and Rod was the number-three man behind the top two executives who were also the company's owners. Rod had a company car, a monthly expense account bigger than my annual salary, and two full-time secretaries. His five-thousand-square-foot house in the hills of California overlooked the lights of Los Angeles.

But all of that was history. He was now working as a part-time custodian in a small Texas town. Part time because his Alcoholics Anonymous sponsor didn't think he could handle more than a few hours of work a week and because he wanted to ensure that Rod didn't miss any meetings. Rod was also living with his girlfriend and waiting for his divorce to become final.

"Just wait till you're my age," he told me during one of his many bouts with depression. "Just wait till life knocks the snot out of you." Rod might have had "the courage to endure," but he lacked "the courage to do."

Like characters in a Hemingway novel, too many people spend their lives just trying to survive, feeling as if they've been birthed into an evil world that's hungry to devour their dreams—a world that defeats them at every turn. They conclude that the best they can hope for is simply to survive. And survival takes all the energy they can muster.

Author Iris Krasnow described the dilemma well:

And so it goes, five steps forward, three steps back. All you can do
is hang on for the ride, a ride that is alternately rough and smooth,
a ride that takes you through bushes and brambles, over jagged
boulders and smooth pebbles, a road where the terrain is never the
same from lope to lope. You swing with it, that's all you can do.[4]

"The courage to endure rather than the courage to do." Ever known anyone who lived like that? Ever lived like that yourself?

Of course not. Such dreadful thoughts are reserved for the lost and lonely and brokenhearted. For those living outside the Christian faith.

Aren't they?

A MYTH TO CHALLENGE

Some years ago I (Frank) was teaching an adult Bible class. Several hundred people of various ages attended every week. I've never had much of a problem sharing my personal struggles with others, and one Sunday morning I became especially transparent. In an effort to make a point, I shared some of my struggles with sin and temptation.

After I dismissed the class, a handful of people immediately made their way to the front, several with tears in their eyes. A line began to form as each person waited to tell me a story or problem or struggle. "I've learned that it's just a daily battle," said one man in his forties. "Some days I do better than others, but taking it one day at a time seems to help."

Some simply shook my hand and moved on without saying a word. One older woman, probably in her eighties, grabbed my hand and pulled me close as she whispered, "Thank you for being so honest. It's so good to know I'm not the only one."

I waited for her to say more, but she only stepped back and stared deep into my eyes, her lips quivering slightly as she perhaps wondered whether I could be trusted. After several seconds she smiled, turned my hand loose, and walked away.

But then one of the church leaders stepped forward. Actually, he *stormed* forward with a well-worn Bible open in his hands. He was eager to read a passage from one of Paul's writings, a passage about overcoming our sinful nature. After reading the passage in full but completely out of context, he slammed his Bible shut. "You may still struggle with temptation," he barked, "but that just shows how immature you are." Then he walked away.

"There is a myth flourishing in the church today," wrote Brennan Manning, "that has caused incalculable harm—once converted, fully converted. In other words, once I accept Jesus Christ as my Lord and Savior, an irreversible, sinless future beckons. Discipleship will be an untarnished success story; life will be an unbroken upward spiral toward holiness."[5]

I hate using the faceless term *the church* because it sounds so conspiratorial. Like some elaborate illuminati making devious decisions behind closed doors. It's like saying "them" and "they" when talking about the people who are in control, even though no one can ever pinpoint who "them" and "they" really are. Sometimes, though, there's no other way to say it.

"The church" has taught us that it's our job to be faithful, it's our responsibility to overcome, it's our duty to be sin free. The burden is on our shoulders to rise above the human condition and win out over our sinful ways.

The church has taught us that it's not okay to struggle, it's not okay to question, it's not okay to simply endure. We have to *overcome*. And if we fail to gain the victory, something is dreadfully wrong with us.

These ideas have been around for as long as anyone can remember, so they're accepted at face value. These teachings are rooted in church history and tradition, so their validity is not questioned. At least by those who are part of the church.

But they *have* been challenged by those who have rejected the church's message. Could it be possible that Ernest Hemingway exposed something we've chosen to ignore? Could Miller and Eliot teach us some things about the human condition that the evangelical church has worked hard to deny?

The church has told us that the way to find God is to *be* better and to *do* better. We've been taught that the thing that keeps God distant is our inadequacy. We must overcome the blight of sin if we want God to bless us, to hear us, to find us worthy. We're taught that if we can't catch God, we're simply not chasing him hard enough.

We're saved by grace, of course, but to be truly accepted by God, we need more than that. To please God, to be really good Christians, we have to overcome our human frailties. Enduring is for nonbelievers and faint-hearted followers, not the faithful few. The faithful learn to overcome.

Isn't it about time we started to challenge this God-forsaken myth?

You and I both know we'll never completely overcome our human nature this side of heaven.[6] Every one of us is like an alcoholic fighting to break free from a crippling addiction. Some struggles in life will haunt us until we die. We will stumble and fall, pick ourselves up, then fall again. Our life of faith will always hit detours. The consistent thing about most of our lives is our dogged inconsistency. There will be many times when the best we can hope for is simply to endure.

You know this is true, and so do I. So why do I feel like a traitor for putting the words on paper? Because, like you, I've been conditioned to think otherwise. The Christian faith is said to lead to righteousness, yet even my best efforts at remaining faithful often lead to nothing more than a pale semblance of goodness.

You and I, while we remain on earth, have the courage to endure but not always the courage to do. There will be days when the best we can hope for on our own is to simply survive, because overcoming is just too dog-gone hard!

Isn't it time we challenged the stories we've been told?

THE POINT *IS* THE STRUGGLE

I (Frank) have friends who jokingly refer to me as a card-carrying grace monkey. I'm not sure what that means, but because I come from a back-ground steeped in legalism, I consider it a compliment.

One of these friends, an older man I love dearly but don't always agree with, cornered me after one of my Bible classes and said, "I know why you lean so far toward the grace camp. It's because you grew up in such a stern religious movement, and now you're recoiling from it. You're on this pen-dulum, and someday you'll swing back toward the middle."

"I'm not sure that's it," I told him, "but it's something to think about."

I didn't take his words as an insult, but I didn't take them lightly either. If my relationship with God is in fact some sort of emotional pendulum, I want to know about it. I took a probing look at my faith and realized that there is a very real dynamic going on between God and me. My relation-ship with him has changed drastically over the past ten years. My view of his mercy and grace is far different now. Something is happening, but a swinging pendulum is not how I would describe it. A tug of war is a much better metaphor.

For many years I've struggled to understand God, to make sense of his ways, to somehow bridge the inconsistencies between what I've been told about him and what I've experienced. I struggle for a higher level of understanding and insight, a broader perspective.

God and I have been in a spiritual and emotional tug of war for as long as I can remember. And the reason I feel closer to him today than I've ever felt is that he has used this struggle to draw me nearer, to woo me into his love. The harder I pull, the closer he draws me, the deeper his goodness flows, and the larger and more real his mercy becomes to me. If I am indeed a card-carrying grace monkey, it is only because God has pulled me to this place in my relationship with him, and I'll proudly wear the label.

That same tug of war is also at work when it comes to my sinful desires. I will never completely overcome my struggle with sin and disobedience. I will try until my last breath, but my humanity will always get in the way and leave me short of my goal. I can no more overcome my human frailties than I can comprehend the deep places of God, yet I can't allow this knowledge to stop me from trying. I can't give up the struggle because the struggle is what most engages me in my relationship with God.

Intimacy is born of struggle. It is a law of the universe, as real as gravity. Without struggle there can be no growth, only stagnation. There is no fire without friction. No forward progress without movement. No answers that aren't rooted in questions. No birth without pain. No relationship with God that doesn't include wrestling with him.

This is what separates you and me from the characters in a Hemingway novel. They are free to give up when life gets confusing and they can no longer endure, but you and I can't do that. We can't give up our struggles because it is through struggling that we find fellowship with God. Through struggle, we develop intimacy with him.

In God's paradigm, overcoming is not expected. If we could overcome in our own strength, then what was the point of the Cross?

Struggle is what engages us in our relationship with God. He looks for our willingness to remain in the struggle, to continue walking with him, fighting to grasp him, resisting the temptation to give in to our human nature, refusing to give up no matter how hard life gets. It is only through struggle that God lifts us up into the Larger Story.

Intimacy is born of struggle.

THE POET BEHIND THE POEM

In the movie *Dead Poets Society,* Robin Williams plays the role of John Keating, a new English teacher at a boys' prep school that is steeped in tradition. In one scene Keating asks one of his students to read aloud from the introduction of their textbook, a section titled "Understanding Poetry" by Dr. J. Evans Pritchard. As the boy reads, Keating takes notes on the chalkboard.

The boy's reading teaches us that poetry, in order to be called poetry, must be fluent in meter, rhyme, and figure of speech and that its composition must contain certain critical elements. In interpreting poetry, strict rules must be followed. And these rules must be carefully analyzed.

While the student reads, Keating graphs all these points on the chalkboard. When the boy finishes, Keating shocks his students by angrily drawing a huge *X* across the notes on the chalkboard. He turns to the class, and in the crudest language he can muster and still not be fired, he says, "Excrement!"

Eyes grow wide and mouths fall open as he continues. "That's what I think of Mr. J. Evans Prichard. We're not laying pipe; we're talking about poetry!"

He then commands the boys to rip the introduction out of their textbooks. "Go on. Rip out the entire page," he tells them. "Rip it out! Rip it out!"

You can feel the tension in the room as one by one the boys do the unthinkable. It feels wrong and scandalous—at the very least improper—but they do it anyway. Slowly at first, then aggressively.

"We shouldn't be doing this," says one frightened young boy.

"Rip it out!" Keating tells him.

After the boys finish and the noise dies down, Keating calms his voice and in a moving "hero" speech, he says,

> Now, in my class you will learn to think for yourselves again.... We
> don't read and write poetry because it's cute. We read and write
> poetry because we are members of the human race. And the human
> race is filled with passion...poetry, beauty, romance, love, these are
> what we stay alive for.... The powerful play goes on, and you may
> contribute a verse.[7]

Keating knew that as a teacher he had two options. He could teach his students to analyze poetry, or he could teach them to experience it. He could show his boys the rules and guidelines that define a poem, or he could usher them inside the mind of the poet. One approach would give them the tools and skills to graph a poem; the other would give them the heart to grasp it.

There are times when the best thing we can do is stop and rip out the introduction, to stop focusing on what we've been told and start listening for what God wants to tell us. To stop reading what others have said about the Christian life and instead look into the heart of the Giver of life.

As scandalous and improper as it may feel, there are times when we need to look beyond the rules and into the Greater Story behind the rules.

A SCANDAL IN THE MAKING

The apostle Paul wasn't always the apostle Paul. Before he crossed paths with Jesus, he was Saul, a Pharisee, a teacher of the Law. He was a rigid zealot who knew as much about God's sacred Rule Book as any man alive. He may not have written the introduction, but he certainly had it memorized. And he did more than teach it; he *enforced* it.

But that was before he knew Jesus. Before he met the Poet. Before he understood the mind and heart behind the poetry of Scripture.

"I consider everything a loss," Paul announced, "compared to the surpassing greatness of knowing Christ Jesus my Lord, for whose sake I have lost all things. I consider them *rubbish,* that I may gain Christ and be found in him, not having a righteousness of my own that comes from the law, but that which is through faith in Christ."[8]

Everything changed for Paul the day the Poet showed up. His encounter with Jesus brought everything into perspective. Paul knew he could never again open the Rule Book without seeing the face behind it or analyze a passage of the Law without feeling the scars of the Writer. He could never again teach a student how to think without first introducing him to the heart and soul of the Master Poet.

"Rubbish!" Paul said. But trust me, he didn't use the ancient Greek equivalent of *rubbish*. Look up the verse in a Bible lexicon and his language might make you blush.[9] Like Keating, Paul needed a strong word to get his point across, so he used the strongest one he could think of. It was the most scandalous testimony imaginable. He compared everything he had "earned"—along with his religious trappings—to excrement.[10] Paul never allowed Gentile believers to be bound by the Law, and he constantly admonished Jewish believers to grasp its fulfillment in Christ. "Rip out the introduction," he was saying. "Go on. Rip it out!"

The Law had been the guidebook for the nation of Israel, the tool for graphing and analyzing a person's standing before God. How else would anyone know how to please God or keep his anger at bay? How else could they understand what he wanted from them? How else could they know what to do to get God's attention? How else could they know how to live so that God would fulfill his promises?

"Rip it out," Paul told them. "We're not laying pipe; we're building a relationship with God!"

As Paul drew his readers to the heart of the Poet, he drew an undignified *X* across everything that had gone before. All the books of the Law and the Prophets hung in the balance as Paul grasped hold of Jesus' revolutionary rules of engagement with God.

"Rubbish!" he told them. "That's what I think of the loveless story of legalism that I lived before I met Jesus."

Two thousand years of church history and tradition have conditioned you and me to think that *overcoming* is the way to God, that God can be pleased only through rules and regulations. But Paul challenges us to rethink this belief.

"What God wants is relationship," Paul is telling us. "He doesn't want us to only analyze the poem; he wants us to get inside the heart of the Poet. God knows that you will never fully overcome; he only expects you to engage in the struggle."

Rules and regulations make the story about us, but the Story is not about us. It never has been! It's all about God.

TRUSTING IN THE STORY OF GOD

When the story is about us, life can be reduced to the courage to endure rather than the courage to do. The best we can hope for is to survive, to do our best to get through the day as sin free as we can. When the story is about us, we are destined to spend our days chasing God, struggling to find him in the midst of our flawed humanity. And for all our chasing, we will inevitably come up empty, because we're analyzing the wrong story.

When the story is about us, much of our life is certain to be spent in fear and worry and internal chaos. When we think about having to face God one day, we will be terrified at the thought of having our innermost sins exposed and judged. When the story is about us, we are likely to be alert in the things of the Story of God, "but *only* in the things, and not the significance."[11] We may see the facts yet miss the ramifications. We may log new information about God, jot down notes in the margins of our Bible, gather new details about his nature and yet never understand the significance of God and his Story.

When the story is about us, we may see the poem, but we will never see the heart of the Poet. That's why the Story is not about us.

The greatest gift God ever gave us was the gift of making the Story completely about him. The most powerful truth in Scripture is that all of Scripture is about God. It is not about you, yet it has everything to do with you.

You and I have been raptured into a Story that is larger and grander and more significant than we could possibly comprehend. We've been caught up in a Romance like no other, and the saddest thing of all is that we seldom look outside of ourselves long enough to see it. Maybe we're too busy living out the small, tired story of our own lives—a story in desperate need of reframing.

A ROMANCE TO EMBRACE

Perhaps the hardest thing you will ever do is accept God's acceptance of you, which leads to resting in the faithfulness of God instead of wallowing in the faith-*less*-ness of your humanity.

If we could learn to trust and rest and *be* instead of always striving to *do*, we would find ourselves face to face with some of life's most perplexing paradoxes. First, that transformation comes only when we stop trying to transform ourselves. Second, that love can flow out of us only after we've allowed it to flow freely into us. And third, that you can't catch God by chasing him; you catch him only by accepting his pursuit of you.

And here is perhaps the greatest paradox of all: God somehow made the Story all about you by not making it about you at all.

PART II

A COURTSHIP TO BE NURTURED

THE PURPOSE THAT KEEPS YOU

*The heart is set free to love extravagantly only
after being caught and exposed.*
—SHARON HERSH

*What I love most about reality is that it's always
the story of a past. And what I love most about
the past is that it's over.*
—BYRON KATIE

In February 2001, scientists announced that the human genome contains not one hundred thousand genes as they had originally thought, but only thirty thousand genes. This revelation may not mean much to you and me, but within scientific circles it amounted to a monumental upset of the status quo. Such a small number of genes could not account for all the different ways people behave. Thus, the debate between nature and nurture was reopened.

"No longer is it nature versus nurture, but nature via nurture…," wrote DNA expert Matt Ridley. "The more we lift the lid on the genome, the more vulnerable to experience genes appear to be."[1]

This monumental discovery helped put to bed the myth that heredity held all the cards over environment. Scientists were forced to reconcile the delicate balance between nurture and nature. The human brain is made for nurture. And that isn't all that needs nurturing.

If you and I are hard-wired to be in relationship with God, created *by* Love and *for* Love, then doesn't that relationship need nurturing? If our identity is wrapped up in God, then how do we open ourselves to the identity that God wrote for us? How do we allow it to transform us?

This is not your ordinary shift in relational dynamics. It's an about-face, a 180-degree turn, a reversal of everything we've been taught about our responsibility toward God. His Story not only compels us to see God in a different light; it exhorts us to live in a different state of mind, to relate to God differently, love him differently, and allow him to love us differently.

And that demands a life dedicated to drawing near to God, but not in order to get him to draw near to us—he has already done that. And not in an effort to please him—he's already pleased with us. And definitely not as a means of activating his love toward us—he already loves us. We draw near to God in order to allow his love to transform us and compel us to cast our eyes higher. He wants to engage us in the divine Courtship that is already underway.

SIX

Your Eternal Identity

Finding the Person God Made You to Be

The chains begin to break when we are willing to
believe we are who God says we are.
—Beth Moore

It is never fitting to say that we are only human.
—Molly Marshall

There is a moment in most of our lives when we begin to ask the big questions, the ones that can't be silenced by the typical canned responses. Questions such as "Who am I?" and "Why am I here?" We're looking not for a name but for an identity, a reason for being. We want to know first if there is a purpose to our life and, second, exactly what that purpose is. The answers we find are critical because they become the foundation for everything we think and believe about ourselves, the world, and God.

In Search of an Identity

I (Tim) don't remember when the big questions first arose in my soul, but I do remember an incident that stirred them to the surface. I was twelve years old and completing the last leg of my daily paper route. I took a quick break to get a candy bar at the grocery store, and in front of me in line stood a woman, probably in her midforties, who was wearing a dark brown, fake leather jacket. She had three carts full of groceries. *Three carts full!* Like she shopped only once a year. It was a small store with only one checkout line open, so I waited as the cashier rang up the woman's items. There were no bar codes to scan in those days, just prices to be punched in one number at a time.

I waited for what seemed an eternity. I could feel my childhood slipping away as the cash register churned and chimed with each new item. *Ching, chung. Ching, chung. Ching, chung.* Did I mention that I had *just one item?*

Finally, the last can of food was placed in a bag, and the woman handed over a check. The cashier glanced at it and said, "I'll need to see some ID." And that's when it happened.

The woman took a step back and glared at the cashier. With all the disgust she could muster, she said, "ID? Why, don't you know who I am? My husband owns the 422 Trailer Park!"

I couldn't believe my ears. Even at the age of twelve, I knew how ridiculous and pathetic that sounded. I'd been taught to be polite, especially to adults, so I tried my best to bite my tongue, but I couldn't do it. I burst out laughing. And it wasn't a chuckle; it was a barrel laugh from the pit of my gut. The cashier heard me, and she started laughing too, quietly at first, then much louder. The laughter was contagious. Soon everyone within earshot was snorting and chuckling. The kid bagging groceries, the woman in line behind me, the man behind her—everyone was laughing at the woman in the fake leather jacket. And she was getting more infuriated by the minute.

I felt bad for what I had started, but I honestly couldn't help myself. I had never heard anything that sounded quite so small and trite. I remember thinking, *I'm not sure who I am, but I know who I'm not.* I knew I would never settle for an identity as insignificant as the person who's married to the person who owns the trailer park off Route 422. Talk about a sad identity!

And yet how often do you and I do the same thing—exchange our true identity for one that's far inferior to who we really are?

KNOW THYSELF

Socrates was walking and talking with his student Phaedrus when the two came to a stream. They decided to take off their sandals and wade into the cool water. While resting on a rock beside the stream, Phaedrus, referring to an ancient Greek legend, asked his teacher, "I should like to know, Socrates, whether the place is not somewhere here at which Boreas is said to have carried off Orithyia from the banks of the Ilissus?"

"Such is the tradition," Socrates told him.

But Phaedrus wasn't content with his answer. "And is this the exact spot?" he asked Socrates.

"I believe that the spot is not exactly here but about a quarter mile lower down," Socrates answered.

Still, his young student wanted to know more. "I beseech you to tell me, Socrates. Do you believe this tale?"

Socrates reluctantly began explaining to his young apprentice that the story had many discrepancies and inconsistencies, making it almost certain that the tale was merely a legend in spite of the fact that many believed it to be true. Then on the heels of his lengthy explanation, he said to his young friend,

> Now I have no leisure for such enquiries; shall I tell you why? I
> must first know myself…to be curious about that which is not
> my concern, while I am still in ignorance of my own self, would
> be ridiculous. And therefore I bid farewell to all this.[1]

Socrates knew instinctively how futile it was to be concerned about ancient legends when he didn't yet understand himself. He spent much of his life trying to bring meaning to his existence, trying to understand his own nature. "Know thyself!" became his battle cry. He wanted to know who he was, whether he had a purpose, and what that purpose was. But he died with the same questions he had lived with.

History is populated with great minds, each taking a different approach to the study of meaning, each attempting to answer a simple question: "Who am I?" And each one falling short.

Freud, Jung, Adler, Plato, Chardin, and many others dedicated their lives to discovering life's purpose. Like Socrates they sought to know themselves, but to some degree they all missed the mark. The best they could come up with was a googolplex of ideas about what causes us to do the things we do because they all failed to recognize one critical truth. And without it, they had no hope of finding true meaning. The crucial truth is this: you and I were created in the image of God.[2]

All other things were created *by* God and *for* God, but you and I were created in the *image* of God. We are nothing less than the highest form of God's creation. When God set out to build a universe, he looked to form and function. But when he created us, he looked within. Without an understanding of this reality at the core of our study of the human condition, we are destined to fall desperately short in finding an answer.

We were created in the image of God. That is our primary identity, and that is the puzzle piece so many have struggled to accept.

THE IMAGE OF GOD

Created in the image of God. What does that mean?

You and I know instinctively what it doesn't mean. It doesn't mean that we were created equal with God's *nature*. God is pure, holy, undefiled by evil. He cannot sin. You and I are impure, unholy, too often defiled by evil. We cannot *not* miss the mark.

God's nature is full of love. Our nature is filled with inconsistencies. According to the apostle Peter, you and I are allowed to "participate in [God's] divine nature,"[3] to share in his goodness through the blood of Jesus. But it doesn't come naturally.

So what, then, does it mean to be created in the image of God? Here's what German theologian Claus Westermann had to say:

> All exegetes from the fathers of the church to the present begin with the presupposition that the text is saying something about people, namely that people bear God's image because they have been created in accordance with it.... But the text is speaking about an *action of God*, and not about the nature of humanity....
>
> What is the purpose of the creator God when he decides to create a person in his image?... The creator decides to create something that is *his own personal concern*....
>
> What God decides to create must be something that has a relationship to him...so that *something can happen between creator and creature*.[4]

Did you catch that? God wasn't talking about *our* nature; he was talking about *his* purpose. The Genesis passage isn't about who we are; it's about whom we are in God's eyes. You and I are God's *own personal concern*. Once again, it's not about our story; it's about God's Story. Doesn't that make more sense?

Too often we've been taught to live in the smaller story of *our* lives, focusing on what we can do in our own power and overlooking the Big Story, the Story of God. But we were created to live in the Larger Story—in God's Story. We are on earth not to work hard at being *like* God but to be in *relationship* with God.

"We are more than our physical urges and needs," wrote Molly Marshall. "Our lives are bent toward our destiny created by God.... We perceive that the mystery of our existence is wrapped up in the mystery of God."[5]

"Who am I?" the greatest minds continue to ask.

And God answers unequivocally, "You were created in my image. You are my own personal concern."

That is an identity worth claiming!

THE ART OF SELF-TRANSCENDING

James Fowler, a professor at Emory University, has written extensively about stages of faith. He argues that people tend to grow in their faith along fairly predictable pathways. Some theologians have called this a process of progressive understanding. Fowler demonstrates how humans can become self-transcending in their relationship with God and with other people simply by increasing their level of spiritual understanding. As our perceptions change, our level of spiritual maturity changes with it—and so do we.

Self-transcending means rising above your own ability, going higher than you could go on your own, growing in ways that are theoretically impossible from a purely human standpoint.

If Fowler is right—and I believe he is—then think of the implications. Because we bear the image of God, we can transcend our human nature and be lifted up into God's nature. That's what Peter meant when he revealed God's invitation for us to become "participants" in God's "divine nature."[6] God wants us to leave behind our small stories and enter into his Larger Story. He wants access to the deepest recesses of our lives so he can transform the way we think and act. He desires to help us reach a level of vulnerability before him and others so that we can grow in our faith. And this takes a level of intentionality that many of us have not attempted.

To self-transcend, to go beyond what is normally thought to be humanly possible, we must transform our way of thinking. First, by changing the way we see God. And second, by changing the way we see ourselves in relationship with God.

AN INTENTIONAL LIFESTYLE

This book was published simultaneously with a companion workbook that walks you through a ninety-one-day journey of reflection. The workbook was no afterthought; it was intentional.

What you hold in your hands is not just another book on the nature of God; it's an effort to breathe a level of intentionality into the community of believers. It's a move toward a more complete and balanced understanding of God's ultimate intention for all of us. It's a fuller telling of God's Story with an emphasis on our place within his life-transforming Story.

In order to self-transcend the distorted and damaging messages of our past, we need to pursue a lifestyle of walking with God, resting in God, being comfortable with God, and talking with God on a daily basis. That doesn't mean we simply find a new way to do everything ourselves or that we assume the responsibility for making sure God stays near. It's actually just the opposite: It means living in the identity God has given us. It's seeing God as the relentless Pursuer and ourselves as the pursued. It's a way of living in which we see ourselves as God's personal concern.

A shift as dramatic as this doesn't happen by accident. It happens through understanding and then by following up that understanding with a changed outlook that steadily transforms our way of living. It takes a new awareness that God desires a deeper, more intimate relationship with us.

And there is one more thing, an additional change in understanding, that must come before you can move forward into your true identity.

The Failure of Fear

A mountain threatens, "If you attempt to climb me, you may fall and die." Yet up the treacherous side of Everest climbers go. Many never make it back.

A tornado says, "If you chase me and get too close, you may get killed." Yet right into the path of the tornado the storm chasers rush. And sometimes their luck runs out.

A cigarette says, "If you smoke me, you will likely get lung cancer." Yet every day kids pick up a pack and learn how to smoke.

An evangelist says, "If you don't come to Jesus, you will burn in hell." Yet in spite of such a dire warning, most of the world refuses to believe.

A pastor says, "If you don't stop sinning, God will punish you." Yet week after week the members of his congregation continue to sin.

Trying to motivate people through fear is like balancing a broomstick on your nose. It takes monumental effort. You might get it to work, but how long can you sustain it? Sooner or later the broom will tip and fall, and you're forced to start all over again. Fear might motivate someone for a short time, but soon it produces guilt and shame that eventually lead to indifference. Yet so many in the church are convinced that fear is the best way to bring about change in people's lives. But the reality is that fear never leads to positive change; it leads to stagnation and resentment.

Fear causes us to withdraw into ourselves. Love lifts us up. Fear intimidates and disgraces. Love nurtures.

There is a way to deal with sin, but fear is not it. You deal with sin through a renewal of heart and mind, through a new and true understanding of what it means to be made in the image of God. You deal with sin through a lifestyle immersed in love.

You and I both know how easy it is to compile a long list of sins and vices. The Bible is filled with examples of every type, every shape, every color, and every flavor under the sun. We could fill several volumes with the things that are an assault on God's nature—and no one would argue that a single item on the list is anything other than wrong. The questions we need to ask, though, are these: How does God deal with our sin? And in light of his response, how should we deal with it?

LIVING AT CROSS-PURPOSES

If we hope to self-transcend in our relationship with God, we need to confront two realities about sin. At first glance these two truths appear to be contradictory, but in reality they are equally important and need to be woven together.

The first truth is that our sins are an affront to God's nature. He hates sin because it's a lifestyle of lovelessness. Sin corrupts and perverts love and leads to even greater lovelessness. It steals from us and leaves nothing but emptiness and devastation in its wake.

The second truth is that God has promised not to equate our sin with our identity. In fact, he says he no longer sees our sins, that he has forgotten them. In spite of all our sin—past, present, and future—we are safe in the blood of Jesus.[7]

The Bible could not be any clearer about these two truths. We all instinctively understand the first one, and we put all our faith in the second one. But how do we get these two realities to coexist? How do you say to a person, "Nothing you do can keep you from the love of God," and in the next breath say, "But you need to stop living as you do"? How do we get to the place where we truly believe that God no longer sees our sins and yet still want to live a life that is as free of sin as possible?

We certainly don't do it through fear. We do it through love, through a true understanding of the love relationship we have with God and how sin affects that relationship.

Molly Marshall described sin as living at "*cross-purposes* with our potentiality as the image of God."[8] Isn't this exactly what sin is—living at cross-purposes with our true identity in Christ? Sin gets in the way of our relationship with God. It detours, distracts, dilutes, strains, undermines—however you want to say it. It stifles the nurturing process in our lives that God is so heavily invested in. We open ourselves up to allow God to transform us, to go deep into the things of our lives, and sin comes along and slows the process. Sin is an affront to God because it is an affront to everything he wants to do within us.

A PRODIGAL'S TALE

Jesus told the story of a man who had two sons. The younger son came to his father and asked for his share of the inheritance. He took his money and traveled to a faraway land where he squandered his inheritance on loose living.

When the son had spent all he had, he hired himself out to a pig farmer. He soon found himself living with the pigs, longing to eat from the same trough. He eventually came to his senses and decided to go back home, but he couldn't imagine that his father would accept him. Not after all he'd done. He told himself, "I will get up and go to my father, and will say to him, 'Father, I have sinned against heaven, and in your sight; I am no longer worthy to be called your son; make me as one of your hired men.' "[9]

The prodigal son made the long journey home, hoping to be accepted back, even if it was just as a lowly servant in his father's household.

You know the rest of the story. Not only was the father waiting for his son, but he ran out to meet him. He embraced and kissed his son, then he clothed his son in his finest robe. He gave him sandals and a ring that signified his position in the family, and then he had a calf killed in honor of his lost son's return.[10]

You could write a dozen books on the analogies that can be drawn from the story of the prodigal son. You and I are the prodigal. We travel to faraway lands in search of something more, even if the journey takes place only in our minds. We squander the good things God has given us. We leave our home with God to look for happiness or comfort or meaning elsewhere.

God is the patient Father, always waiting at the gate for his wayward children to return.

The prodigal son had everything he needed at home, all the love he could ask for, all the comfort he could imagine. Yet something in his nature compelled him to wander. He chose to seek his identity elsewhere. And his seeking did nothing more than lead him into a pigpen. He was living at cross-purposes with his true identity as his father's son. The wealthy son of a loving king found himself working as a slave and living with pigs because he forgot who he was. But his father never forgot.

To his father, the prodigal was a wayward son who simply needed to find his way home. A son who was too far away to see how much he was loved. A son who was too distant to be nurtured by his father. That's why the father stood waiting at the gate. His son's bed was empty, and the father's heart longed to have his child back home where he belonged.

All of us at one time or another try to find our identity in a faraway land. Some of us simply travel farther and longer and more often than others. When we search for love or acceptance or approval anywhere outside of our home with God, we are destined to live with pigs. But being separated from God's nurturing care tends to bring us around. We eventually come to our senses and decide to come back home. In shame and remorse we approach the gate. And with our heads bowed and our eyes lowered, we say to our Father, "I've sinned. I'm not worthy of your love."

But our sacred Pursuer wraps us in his finest coat, slips the ring of kinship onto our finger, and says, "That's nonsense. Don't even talk like that." He throws his loving arms around us, orders his servants to kill the fatted calf, and then leads us up the walkway to enjoy a celebration.

In this story we not only see ourselves in the actions and choices of the prodigal, but we vividly see portrayed the nature of the Father's heart—a heart that furiously pursues his children, who will forever find their identity as his sons and daughters.

"My child, who was lost, is now back home," the Father says. "You may have forgotten who you were, but I never did."

SEVEN

GOD'S SINGLE-MINDED COURTSHIP

WON OVER BY GOD'S FURIOUS PURSUIT

> My assumption is that the story of any one of
> us is in some measure the story of us all.
> —FREDERICK BUECHNER

> But in order to make you understand, to give
> you my life, I must tell you a story.
> —VIRGINIA WOOLF

I s there anything in life that can move hearts like a story? The stories we tell, for better or worse, largely determine our view of reality and our approach to life, love, and relationship.

Your life is a story. My life is a story. And the book we call the Bible is a story. It is God's Story, meant to be the guiding Story for us all.

The Story of God is the story of a sacred Creator in furious pursuit of his creation, a Pursuer who never relents, never tires, never gives up on his beloved. It's the Story of a God who becomes flesh in order to do for us what we could never have done on our own. And this thing God did for us, this "God's doing," really is the whole point.

When we begin with the story of ourselves, we're tempted to think that the Big Story is about us. We start to believe that we're responsible for bringing about a happy ending, that in some small but desperate way the plot resolution is up to us.

Yet nothing could be further from the truth. And knowing that the plot resolution is not up to us is the primary message of the Bible.

We can each see ourselves—our good days and our bad days—somewhere in the pages of Scripture. From Adam to the apostle John, we see the characters of the Bible struggling to live out their faith, struggling daily with their humanity, constantly walking the fine line between soil and spirit, between dirt and divinity. We relate to the characters in Scripture because they are living out our story.

But the Greater Story, the Story of God, is one that none of us can really relate to. Maybe that's why it's so hard to accept. God's furious pursuit is far beyond anything you and I could ever comprehend.

We all know that God is holy, but what does *holy* mean? The primary definition is "other than," and what could possibly be more "other" than God and his Story—and what he does with the story of our lives?

LOOKING FOR LOVE

Every one of us wants to feel unique and special. We all want to be desired, even if we only experience the intense affection of just one other person. We want to be *wanted*. It's built into our DNA. Each of us wants a one-on-one relationship. We don't always find it, but most of us will keep searching until we do.

I (Tim) have a vivid memory of my first day in college. I had just finished registering for classes and was milling around in the student center when suddenly a beautiful girl walked up and said, "Tim King, how are you?"

I didn't recognize her, but I wasn't about to keep walking. "Great, how are you?" I answered, trying to remember who she was.

"Don't you recognize me?" she said. "I'm Belinda. We met at freshman orientation."

I still didn't remember, but I pretended that I did. "Oh yeah. Belinda, good to see you again."

We talked for several minutes, mostly about registration and dorm rooms and other predictable college conversation. And then, not wanting to miss a golden opportunity, I said, "You know, they're playing a movie on campus this Friday night. Would you like to go?"

"That sounds fun," she said. "Where do you want to meet?"

We made the arrangements, exchanged phone numbers and dorm information, and I went on my way feeling about two feet taller. I walked back to my room thinking, *How cool is this? My first day of college, and I've already got a date!*

I had grown up in a small town with a church youth group made up of about six kids—half were boys and the other half may as well have been. We were all close friends, like family. I couldn't remember the last time I'd had a date, and I was going out with the prettiest girl I'd seen on campus. I suddenly understood why it took my older brothers so long to graduate.

As soon as I got back to my dorm, I started bragging to my roommate. I told him about meeting a girl and about my date Friday night. Then he said, "That's strange. The same thing happened to me. I met a girl today, and we're going out this Saturday night."

"Really," I said, and he told me all about it. He'd met her at registration and struck up a conversation, and the next thing he knew, they had set a date to go out to dinner.

"What's her name?" I asked.

"Belinda."

Now that's a coincidence, I thought.

The two of us talked further and realized we were going out with the same girl—he on Saturday and me on Friday. Talk about awkward. *And deflating.* But that wasn't even the strangest part. As we discussed our dilemma, wondering about the odds of something like this happening, a friend down the hall came bursting into our room grinning from ear to ear. He said, "You won't believe what just happened. I met the most incredible girl. She's gorgeous, and we're going out tonight! Here it is the first day of college, and I've already got a date."

"Let me guess," I said. "Her name is Belinda."

I meant it as an inside joke between my roommate and me. But our friend said, "How'd you know?"

Sure enough, it was the same girl. We stood there feeling like three retread tires and wondering whether there was a fourth rolling around somewhere on campus, waiting to complete the set. We'd all just made a date with the girl of our dreams, each convinced we'd discovered our soul mate, only to realize that we'd done little more than meet the one girl on campus addicted to free food. We wondered if she'd set a date with every guy in the dorm. Maybe right then she was standing at the front door passing out coupons.

That day I went from feeling on top of the world to picking dirt out of my teeth. They don't build a roller coaster that can drop that fast. One minute I felt like the most special person on the planet, the hunkiest guy on campus, and the next minute I was just one of the pack. From Mr. Right to Mr. Take-a-Number.

ONE AMONG MANY?

Have you ever felt that you were just one among many? Just a name and a number walking around a planet filled with billions of other names and numbers? Have you ever wondered if that's how God sees you—just another anonymous acorn falling from the tree of life, struggling to take root and grow?

Have you ever wondered why we feel that way?

You and I were born into a culture—even a church culture—influenced by the modern age, an era that has produced too many wonderful advances to even attempt to count. We've progressed in medicine, transportation, finance, science, manufacturing, and health. And that doesn't even touch on the *really important* advances, such as microwave popcorn, TiVo, and drive-through windows at Starbucks!

These advances have made life interesting, but there's a downside. The modern age has done more than change the way we live; it's changed the way we think—and not always in a good way. The modern age is an age of industry and commerce, an age of mass production, assembly lines, robotics, and mass communication. It's the age of faster, more, better, cheaper;

an age of efficiency and profitability, no matter the cost. It isn't enough to make a better widget; you have to make it faster and at less cost to increase margins and pay higher dividends to shareholders. And soon, even the best and most advanced widget becomes obsolete and is discarded.

When you're in the business of modern-age mass production, some things are simply expendable. They're not worth wasting your time on, so you chuck them and get on with your day. But somewhere along the way, the concept of accelerated obsolescence began to apply not just to products but also to people. We became expendable. We're not "employees" or "workers" anymore; we're "human resources." We're widgets making widgets. And sometimes a human widget comes along who's worth more than the previous one, so you discard the current one to make room for a better one.

We live in a culture that most highly values speed, efficiency, profit, progress, and market share. So why wouldn't God see us that way—as if we're just one little widget among billions of widgets? Worse yet, maybe we're the damaged widget. God is bound to notice that we're worth far less than all the other widgets. So why wouldn't he just discard us and move on to a better one?

But the approach and assumptions of the modern age are not at all consistent with the Story of the Bible. Scripture relates the Story of a Creator who not only creates but pursues his creation with inexhaustible passion.

In Ezekiel 16, God promises to restore Israel.[1] This restoration will follow a season of neglect, suffering, poverty, and isolation. And isn't such a restoration what we all hope for? The widespread image of a God of vengeance and judgment is the easy picture to hold on to, but it's not the God of the Big Story. All you have to do is read the Old Testament in context to see that the God of the Bible is a God not of wrath but of mercy and forgiveness and restoration. God's Story is a Love Story. Nothing else.

And right in the middle of God's Story is one of the most dramatic stories of love and redemption ever written, not just in Scripture but in the history of the world. It is a story so potent, so "other than" anything we've ever imagined to be true, that theologians have been tempted to call it an allegory. Surely nothing this outlandish could happen in real life.

From this story in the pages of Scripture, God screams out to us, "I don't judge you; neither do I minimize your value and importance. That is not who I am!"

It's the story of Hosea and Gomer.

LOVE AMPLIFIED

Hosea was a prophet who lived around the eighth century BC, a confusing time in the history of Israel. At the time, the nation of Israel was trying to keep its relationship with God intact while still cutting deals with the surrounding nations. Like us, the Israelites wanted to have their cake and eat it too, always keeping one eye on God and the other on worldly pleasures and gains. Hosea was a prophet, but not one of God's leading men.

As early as 1200 BC, you could find any number of schools in Israel teaching men how to be prophets.[2] Like today's preacher-training schools, these early schools of prophecy would teach men how to speak on God's behalf. Some prophets received a direct prophecy from God and would "foretell" events, while others would simply "forth tell," which means to preach or admonish on God's behalf. Some were inspired by God, given direct words and messages from God. But most of them simply became preachers, reading and teaching the Word throughout Israel.

I've always imagined Hosea as a young, uninitiated prophet barely out of seminary. He was ready to do great things for God, to go wherever God sent him, to be a mighty force in Israel. He had no idea what God had in store for him, and then suddenly out of nowhere he heard God's voice. He was about to get his first big project. "I'm ready, Lord," he said. "Just tell me what you want me to do!"

And then he learned his assignment. "I want you to marry a prostitute,"[3] God told him. God commanded Hosea to love the unlovable one, to marry a promiscuous, unfaithful woman.

You can see why so many people have a problem with this story. It doesn't sound like something God would do. Ask a good and decent man to marry a harlot? Pair a prophet and a prostitute? I've seen spaghetti westerns that made more sense, and yet that's exactly what God told Hosea to do.

"Go, take to yourself an adulterous wife and children of unfaithfulness, because the land is guilty of the vilest adultery in departing from the LORD."[4]

God was asking no small thing. We know that God takes marriage very, very seriously because marriage gives us greater insight into the nature of God. First and foremost, marriage is a sacred union. It is a divinely ordained coming together of two people in the most intimate of all human relationships. It's two people making a solemn and singular covenant with each other before God and the world. There's nothing casual about it; it's a binding promise.

Second, marriage demands an investment of self. It's a commitment of time, energy, and resources—an individual commitment to be there no matter what. This is no long-distance relationship; it is a hallowed trust, a covenant of personal presence.

Third, marriage is one on one. It's not a corporate merger; it's between two people, a husband and wife, clinging to each other through ups and downs and in-betweens, through everything that life throws their way. It's a melding of mind, body, and spirit. In a very mystical and spiritual sense, it is two becoming one.

God could not be clearer about the importance of marriage. And in light of this, isn't it interesting that God would use the marriage between Hosea and Gomer to illustrate his relationship with you and me? Why would he symbolize his eternal commitment to us through the story of a marriage between an obedient prophet and an unfaithful, unlovable harlot?

It's not that far-fetched. Marriage is a perfect picture of how God sees us in his Larger Story. Our relationship with him is a sacred union. It is completely "other than" anything we could ever imagine.

It also is a personal investment of the highest order on God's part. He is eternally invested in his relentless pursuit of our hearts.

And it is a one-on-one relationship. God doesn't see us as a dorm full of guys, each setting a date with the same needy woman. Each of us has a one-on-one relationship with him. Through the story of Hosea and Gomer, God is telling us, "This relationship is all about you and me."

But where are we in their story?

Unholy Delusion

It didn't take Gomer long to live down to Hosea's expectations. And, like Gomer, it often doesn't take you and me very long to live down to God's expectations.

Even though Gomer had three children with Hosea, her heart and mind quickly drifted to other lovers. But Hosea's love never wavered. His only desire was to woo back his wandering wife. No amount of sexual infidelity on Gomer's part could destroy his love and desire for her.

Imagine what Hosea's friends must have thought. *Poor ol' Hosea. Can't pick a wife, can't keep a wife, can't muster the self-respect to turn her loose.*

Then, revving up the gossip mill to full throttle, Gomer decided to move back home as if nothing out of the ordinary had happened. "I might as well return to my husband," she reasoned, "because I was better off with him than I am now."[5]

Unbelievable! Can you imagine the presumption in that attitude? The unmitigated gall of even thinking, much less doing, such a thing? Gomer ran off and gave her body to other men. Then she ran out of money and thought, *I guess I'll go home now because I was better off with Hosea.* From her perspective, her relationship with Hosea was based solely on what was best for her.

Don't you wish you had a stone?

It's easy to get incensed as you read the story, until you remember that it's *our* story. You and I do the same thing almost daily in our relationship with God. How many times do we check out, choosing to live at cross-purposes with our true identity in Christ? How frequently do we run off to a faraway land and live with pigs, and then later decide, *I'm not living right. I need to move back in with God*? How many days do we allow our hearts to wander, allow our eyes to stray to other lovers, let ourselves be enticed by the empty whispers of materialism, lust, greed, and pleasure, only to later decide to let God take us back?

Do we have any idea how presumptuous that is, what an insult it is to God?

We are quick to trample the grace of God, to take his goodness and mercy for granted. We come back to him after we've tired of our waywardness and assume that he'll be there. We don't give a second thought to the magnitude of his grace, the sheer enormity of love that it takes for him to be willing to accept us back after our promiscuity.

If ever a story demonstrated the furious pursuit of God toward us, it's the marriage of the prophet and the prostitute. If we have ever doubted the depth of God's resolve, the height of his love, the length of his mercy, the width and breadth of his grace in the face of an ungrateful lover, this story lays every doubt to rest. Our unholy presumption is the ultimate challenge to the faithfulness of God. And how God responds in the face of our unfaithfulness is the Story we are called to embrace.

I Give You My Worst

God is a covenant keeper—that's what he does. It is an integral part of his divine nature: he is infinitely faithful, true, and loving.

You and I are covenant breakers—that's what we do. It is a frustrating yet basic part of our nature. We are predictably unfaithful, untrue, unloving.

We break covenant so often that in many ways we don't even recognize it for what it is. We break covenant not only in the things we do but in the things we should be doing but don't. Scholars talk about the sins of omission, but James simply calls it what it is: knowing the good we ought to do and yet not doing it.[6]

The magnitude of our self-absorption is staggering when you include the many times we could have loved but chose instead to be indifferent. It would be mind-boggling if we could measure the countless ways in which we live at cross-purposes with God by focusing on ourselves instead of the needs of others.

God gives us his best; we give him our worst. That just about sums up the nature of our relationship with him. Like Hosea and Gomer, we find ourselves caught up in the most unlikely union imaginable. And still, God remains steadfast.

Therefore I am now going to allure her;
    I will lead her into the desert
    and speak tenderly to her.

There I will give her back her vineyards,

and will make the Valley of Achor a door of hope.[7]

This is how a holy God responds to the waywardness, the indifference, the unholy presumption of his lover. He allures you into the wilderness of the desert. He reaffirms that this is a one-on-one relationship, that you are his sole desire. His love is constant and true and eternally loyal. He takes you aside so that it is just the two of you. There are no outside voices, no distractions, just a Lover and his beloved. Once you are alone, he speaks tenderly to you.

It is the exact opposite of what we might anticipate, certainly not what we expect a divine Lover to say to us in the midst of our transgression. In our earthly paradigm, the wilderness is a perfect place for God to unload, to get even, to unleash his anger in order to get our attention. The desert is a fitting place for him to remind us of the depths of our sin in the midst of his unwavering faithfulness. But that's not what he does. He instead speaks tenderly to us. He shows us nothing but compassion.

God says, "There I will give her back her vineyards, and will make the Valley of Achor a door of hope."[8]

The Valley of Achor is a land of trouble, a place where hope is in short supply. It's where you and I end up when we've run off to a faraway land and made our home with the pigs. It's where we are when our lives become cross-purposed with our true identity. It's where our friends say, "I told you so," and we say, "I got what I deserved." But not God. God says, "Let me show you the door of hope."

Why would God do that? Because his passion runs deep, and the only thing that can boil over is love.

Don't miss this truth. If God's primary character trait were wrath—and we all know how many have tried to convince us of that—then wrath is what we would reap when God responds to our disobedience, our presumption, our arrogance, and our unfaithfulness. But that's not what happens. When God is distressed over our rejection of him, he unleashes nothing but love, because love is God's driving force.

God *is* Love, and his love leads to forgiveness. But God doesn't stop with forgiveness—that's only the beginning. After forgiving us, he restores our hope. Like Hosea wooing back his faithless wife, God gives us back our vineyards. He renews the dignity we so easily squandered.

God waits always at the gate, searching the horizon for our return. And when we come to the end of ourselves and return home, he slips the ring back on our finger, covers us with his finest coat, adorns our feet with sandals, and makes us the guest of honor at a wild celebration. He does more than accept us back; he restores our self-respect. The relationship goes on, not as if nothing had ever happened, but more deeply and meaningfully because of what has happened.

A COURTSHIP OF ONE

Is it possible that God could really see us that way? Isn't this Story a little too good to be true? Surely God's love and grace have limits we aren't able to see. If God is infinitely sacred and holy, and we are so unfaithful and presumptuous, then how can we possibly believe that he would just accept us back?

David struggled endlessly to comprehend the faithfulness of God, and we see from one of his psalms that he was eventually able to grab hold of it, at least on some level:

Where can I go from your Spirit?
　Where can I flee from your presence?

If I go up to the heavens, you are there;

    if I make my bed in the depths, you are there.

If I rise on the wings of the dawn,

    if I settle on the far side of the sea,

even there your hand will guide me,

    your right hand will hold me fast.[9]

He finally came to a place in his life when he ignored the screaming voices of judgment and doubt and allowed God's wilderness whisper to seep through.

David, even if you make your bed in the depths, I am there with you.

How many of us have ever made our bed in the depths, far from our relationship with God?

David, even if you settle on the far side of the sea, even there my hand will guide you. My right hand will hold you fast.

Have you ever run from God? Have you ever found yourself so lost, so far from God, that you needed a guiding hand to hold you fast?

Jonah ran from God when he was commanded to prophesy to the despised Ninevites. But God didn't let him get away. God chased Jonah all the way to the bottom of the ocean in order to bring him home. What makes you think God won't chase you to the end of your iniquity so that he can remind you of his pledge of love?

God doesn't take this Courtship lightly. He's not willing to leave his relationship with you to chance. His covenant is no idle promise. In the midst of your darkest sin, God takes you by the hand. He leads you into the wilderness, looks deeply into your eyes, and whispers, "Don't look away anymore. It's just you and me now. I love you. I always have, and I always will.

"Let's go home…"

EIGHT

LIVING IN THE ETERNAL MOMENT

KNOWING GOD IN THE PRESENT TENSE

Our Lord God is to me all in all. Since he is, what
more would I have and what more can I desire?
—THOMAS À KEMPIS

Today the heart of God is an open wound of love.
He aches over our distance and preoccupation.... He
weeps over our obsession with muchness and
manyness. He longs for our presence.
—RICHARD FOSTER

Time as we know it is an illusion. It may feel real, but it's not. Time is all in your head. Just a figment of your imagination, so much smoke and mirrors.

But you and I live in a world that worships time. We live and die by it. We cling to our Day-Timers or PDAs like a drowning man clinging to a life raft. Time is our lifeline to reality, our tether to the rest of society.

Our preoccupation with linear time wasn't an issue until about the seventeenth century. Before that, the world was pretty much ruled by seasons. There was a season to sow, another to reap, still another to store. Time was measured in much larger chunks, and people weren't married to their schedules.[1]

Somewhere along the way all that changed, but who knows why? Legend has it that Columbus stepped off his ship and bought a watch, and things have never been the same since. Whatever happened, at some point we started obsessing over time. We had to stay on time and make time last, and in the process, we lost touch with the present. We forgot how to live in the moment. And when you lose touch with the present, you lose touch with God, because that's the only place he can exist for you.

God doesn't live according to a time line, because that's just an illusion. God is both the Alpha and the Omega, the Beginning and the End, all at the same time. We are bound by time; God is not.

Down the street from my (Tim's) house is a seafood restaurant with a huge sign painted on the side of the building that reads "Free Crab Legs Tomorrow!" To this day the restaurant has never had to serve a free crab leg because it's never tomorrow.

You can't walk with God in the past or the future; you can only walk with him today, in the here and now. God can meet you only in the present moment.

AN UNCHALLENGED BELIEF

We are all affected by an underlying belief that robs us of our relationship with God. It is the reason we struggle so hard to hear him. It causes our relationships with family and friends to suffer, it creates unnecessary stress, and it robs us of hope.

This underlying belief isn't about our obsession with time, although it has something to do with that. It also isn't about our inability to live in the present, although it has a lot to do with that. It's much more subtle. And it's *always* at work within us.

This underlying belief is that we are not enough and that we don't have enough.

This fear-based belief causes us to be obsessed with time. It's the reason we're so preoccupied with our schedules, so intent on maximizing each hour and each day, so obsessed with performance and productivity. It drives us to live in the future, and it causes us to be eaten up with regret over the past. We all are dogged by the feeling that we're not enough. We believe we're not enough because we don't have enough and we're not accomplishing enough.

Last week I (Frank) met a woman who epitomized this belief. I had an ATV for sale, and she came over with her daughter to look at it. They were at my house only a short time, but she couldn't stop talking about herself— how busy she was, how successful she was, all the things she had accomplished. She talked about the business she owned and how hard she had worked to build it, her plans for expansion, how many employees she had, how tired she was because she hadn't been getting any sleep.

This woman was living with one foot in the past and the other in the future, but she was completely out of touch with the present moment. She was so caught up in the things she had done and the things she planned to do that she couldn't stop long enough to carry on a normal conversation.

At first I was annoyed with her, but then I wondered, *Is she really that different from the rest of us? Is she that far outside the norm?* Could it be that the primary difference between her and me is that she can't stop verbalizing her angst over her status in life and I just keep my angst to myself?

We're so often convinced that everything we need for happiness is "out there" somewhere, just beyond our reach. And we're always striving to get to the place where we can capture the happiness that eludes us. *I've got to chase bigger clients, move more product, get a nicer house, build this church, put my kids through college, save for retirement, find a cure for cancer!* Everything is defined by what we need to accomplish in order to fulfill the purpose we envision for ourselves.

This belief that we are not enough and don't have enough feeds our obsession with time, but it is so ingrained that we don't even notice it. This belief is so much a part of the human psyche that we've lost sight of who we are in the present moment.

Faraway Eyes

God reveals himself to us in the present. But because of our obsession with time, we live constantly either in regret about the past or in fear and worry about the future. We fail to live in the present—the only time zone in which God makes himself known to us.

God has invested everything—all he is and all he has—in nurturing our relationship with him, but we're so caught up in ourselves that we hardly even notice. We're so focused on what we don't have and what we haven't accomplished that we never take time to see what's right here with us—God.

Our underlying belief that we are not enough and don't have enough boils down to ingratitude. God created us *in his image,* but we want to be more than that. He constantly provides all we need, yet we spend our lives wanting more. He longs to live with us in the present, but we can't stop looking to the past or the future. He sees us as his own personal concern and wants a one-one-on relationship with us, but we're hung up on performance, obsessing over all the things we need to accomplish.

Think about God's side of this neglected relationship. We've all tried to carry on a conversation with someone who wasn't "there" with us. Just the other day I (Frank) was talking with my son, David, about one of his friends. This kid impressed me the first time I met him. He finished high school at sixteen and now takes college courses and works as a summer intern at a local ministry.

"You and he don't hang out together much, do you?" I asked my son.

"Not really," David said. "He's okay, but we don't have that much in common."

I was surprised because I thought they had a *lot* in common. They're the same age, both are homeschooled, and both are high achievers who share many of the same friends and interests. I pressed the issue, and David finally said, "Lance isn't that easy to get close to. Whenever you talk to him, he never looks at you. He's always looking around the room to see if there's someone else he'd rather be talking with."

Ever been there? I have. In fact, my wife accuses me of doing the same thing, and she's right. I'm such a people person, such a "party animal," that I often forget to just relax and enjoy the people I'm with.

I also forget to just relax and enjoy being with God. And don't we all?

To this day I (Tim) am convinced that the most spiritually enlightened member of my family, the most "present" one among us, was my recently departed dog, Taffi. Near as I could tell, she never once thought about tomorrow, never once worried about yesterday, never once thought she didn't have enough. All she wanted out of life was to hang out with the people she loved. Present tense. She wanted to love and be loved in the here and now.

If you think I've lost it because I'm suggesting we can learn from a family pet, think again. "Consider the ravens," Jesus said. "They do not sow or reap, they have no storeroom or barn; yet God feeds them. And how much more valuable you are than birds!"[2] Maybe Taffi was onto something after all.

Could it be that what you and I need most is a new way of looking at our lives in the presence of God? Let's try this one on for size: "In this moment, I find God. In this moment, I have all I need."

GETTING YOUR CLOCK CLEANED

I (Frank) used to box in high school. Actually, I should say that I used to "get boxed" because I was never very good at the sport. I had a bad habit of dropping my gloves and leading with my face. Once I went into the ring with a kid half my size and felt pretty confident I could take him. That is, until he came out swinging. It was like trying to fight a windmill. His arms were flailing wildly, coming at me from all directions. He caught me on the nose, and I dropped like a sack of cement. I blacked out for about ten seconds, and when I came to, I had no idea where I was or how I got there. I had lost all track of time.

Coach Coe called this "getting your clock cleaned." It means "getting KO'd," "seeing stars." However you say it, it all leads to the same thing—

a sudden jolt of reality. One minute you're dancing on your toes, planning your next move, adrenaline in high gear, and the next you're flat on your back wondering what day it is.

There's nothing like getting your clock cleaned to bring you kicking and screaming into the present moment. Maybe that's what we need from time to time in our relationship with God—a jolt of reality. What my old boss used to call "getting the rules explained to you."

Jonah didn't own a watch, but he knew the meaning of getting his clock cleaned. If anyone ever lost sight of being present with God, it was Jonah. His book is only four chapters long, and three of them describe Jonah's struggle to control his time line. He was usually either running away from God, running back to God, or running ahead of God. Only one chapter out of four shows Jonah running with God—just 25 percent of the time.

And where did all his running get him? Jonah ended up in the belly of a giant fish in the bottom of the ocean. Marinating in digestive juices, he got his clock cleaned. And only then did he choose to step into the present. But that's what saved him, because only in the present moment could he walk with God.

Then there's Jacob. At one point Jacob was struggling to control his destiny. He was searching for a wife, scrambling to save himself from his brother Esau, working to keep his herds and servants in the right place at the right time, and through it all, to somehow force God's hand in fulfilling his promise of fortune and family. Jacob was running out of room in his Day-Timer as he tried to keep all this stuff straight. God found that he couldn't get Jacob's attention, so he caught him alone one night and decided to explain the rules to him. He wrestled with Jacob from dusk until dawn.[3]

God had big plans for Jacob. Through his seed the world would be blessed. But before that could happen, Jacob needed to learn how to live in the present. He had to hear the rules governing how to walk with God moment by moment. So God cleaned Jacob's clock.

Maybe that's what you and I need. Not a wrestling match with God, just a good jolt of reality regarding our view of time.

THE MYTH OF TIME

We're conditioned to seeing time as a line that begins at some point in our past, runs through today, and then fades into the future. We see it as a train that left the station long ago and continues moving always toward the horizon. And for most of us, it's a runaway train.

We believe the myth that time is a delivery system that takes us from where we started to where we need to be. But what happens when we couple the myth of time with the lie that we're not enough and that we don't have enough? Link the two and the result is a worldview that says, "You only have so much time to become what you need to become and to attain what you need to attain, so you have to move quickly." We become obsessed with *being more* and *doing more,* and then we rush to do it now before we run out of time. We pursue a life of gathering more and producing more so that we can feel like we're worth more.

In the process, our relationships suffer. We lose touch with friends, relatives, neighbors, and even our spouse and children. Our churches start to feel more like weekly PTA meetings than a church family. And worst of all, our relationship with God becomes fractured and distant. What little time we spend in prayer is filled with dread and worry over the future, with stress brought on by our overcommitted lives, with pleas that God will help us be more and do more so that we can attain more. And we suffer as a result.

So let's refuse the myth that time is only linear and the lie that we aren't enough and don't have enough. The speeding train we think we're on doesn't exist. The only time that exists is the present, the here and now, this moment. It is physically impossible to live in any moment other than the present one.

And in spite of what we've been conditioned to think, we *are* enough, and we *have* enough. You and I are created in the image of God. He has provided all we need, and he promises to continue doing so throughout eternity. What else could we possibly need? What else could we possibly need to be?

It's worth repeating: In this moment, I find God. In this moment, I have all I need.

HOPE DEFERRED

When I (Tim) was about thirteen years old, I realized that I needed to get a minibike. It was critical to my future, vital to maintaining the fragile social status that I had worked so hard to achieve. This was no passing whim; I *needed* this minibike for survival.

But my dad didn't see it that way. He refused to buy me one—that is, until he saw that I wasn't going to relent. He finally agreed, but only if I was willing to save the money from my daily paper route.

This sounded like a great idea until I realized how long that was going to take, so I again went to Dad. "Just loan me the money, and I'll pay you back," I told him. "I promise I will!"

Once again he refused, but I wasn't about to give up. It took several weeks, but I eventually wore him down. "Fine," he said one day out of sheer frustration. "Get in the car, and let's get this over with!"

When we got to the store, there on the showroom floor was the most magnificent minibike I'd ever seen. It was silver and black with long chrome handlebars and white sidewall tires. It was a thing of beauty, and I couldn't take my eyes off it. Here before me was the one thing in the world that would finally bring true meaning and contentment to my life. This was my purpose, my destiny! But the salesman wouldn't let us have the one on the floor. Instead, he sold us a box full of parts and explained that we'd have to assemble it ourselves. *Minor detail,* I thought.

When Dad loaded it into the trunk, I was so excited that I took out the handlebars and sat in the backseat all the way home pretending I was driving. I could see myself blazing through the neighborhood, my friends cheering me on, girls waving as I drove by. My life would never be the same.

Dad spent all afternoon helping me put the minibike together, and I nagged him the entire time. "Are you almost finished? Can I ride it yet?"

"Just be patient," he kept telling me, but I couldn't. I was too excited. Finally he put the last part in place and tightened the last nut. Then he wiped the sweat from his brow and told me he was going into the house for a drink. "Now don't do anything, Tim. I'll be back in a minute," he said.

But I couldn't wait another minute. All it needed was a little gas, so I filled up the tank and rolled the minibike into the driveway. I yanked the starter cord, and the engine roared to life on the first pull. It was the most beautiful sound I'd ever heard.

I hopped on, slipped it into gear, then took off down the sidewalk. I felt just like Evel Knievel. Just like that *Easy Rider* guy who rode a Harley in the movie I'd heard about but was too young to watch. I was king of the world, master of my own fate, blazing through life with the wind in my hair and all my cares behind me. I was all of that and more—for about ten yards. That's when something in the motor sputtered and the wheels locked up, leaving a long black streak on the pavement. I flew over the handlebars and rolled end over end right into the neighbor's lawn. And my bike came crashing down onto the hard pavement.

I had forgotten to fill the crankcase with oil. Actually, I didn't know what a crankcase was or that it needed oil, until Dad explained it to me later. And was he ever ticked!

I was so wrapped up in getting what I wanted that I nearly ruined my new minibike. I felt like time was limited, that the future wouldn't wait another minute. I had to hurry up and get there. I was so wrapped up in claiming my destiny as a biker that I completely lost track of the present. I couldn't just live in the moment.

We all get caught up in future glory and unrealized expectations. We set our sights down the road so far ahead of us that we lose sight of the here and now.

"Hope deferred makes the heart sick,"[4] said the wisdom writer. Yet how often do you and I live in a terminal state of deferred hope? We're always looking to the future for fulfillment, always looking "out there" for something we think we need. And before we know it, our future is our past, and we're still not satisfied.

My dad was able to get my minibike running again, but it wasn't long before the thrill was gone, and my little silver and black ticket to destiny was no longer as fulfilling as it once was. I had already begun setting my sights on an even bigger and better bike.

THE POWER OF REGRET

"Hope deferred makes the heart sick." But deferred hope isn't the only thing that prevents us from living in the present moment.

I (Frank) hired Sam to do some detailed painting work on a house my wife and I remodeled, and we were thrilled with the job he did. He took his time to do it right, but all the while it was obvious that his mind was elsewhere.

While he painted, Sam dreamed of all the things he wished he could be doing and the things he should have done with his life. He told us of his days in college and his plans to finish his BA and then attend law school. But then he made the mistake of dropping out and going to work for his dad. "I should have stuck with it," he said. "Do you know how much lawyers make?" From what we were paying, I'm sure Sam was doing fine, but that's not how he saw it.

He spoke of the house he once owned in California and the error he made by selling it too early in a rising market. "Do you know what that house would be worth today?"

He talked about his kids and his plans to see that they made it through college. "I don't want them to make the same mistakes I made," he said. "I want them to make something of themselves."

Sam lived in a perpetual state of regret. He was so eaten up with missed opportunities that he couldn't see what he had going for him. He had a beautiful family, a great business, good health, and incredible skill, not to mention an entire life ahead of him. Most people would envy Sam's position in life, but he didn't see it that way. He felt like a failure because he chose to live in the past.

Regret looms over our heads like an ominous cloud, constantly reminding us of all the things we should have done, all the time we've wasted, all our unrealized hopes. We live with remorse over things we've done or failed to do. Disappointment looms large above all of us. And we give it unwarranted power over our lives.

Writing this chapter uncovered an ammo dump of emotion regarding my own past failures and missed opportunities. We all have a long list of things that quickly rise to the surface when we start talking about the past. Some years back I wasted more than a year of my life regretting some bad investments I'd made. When the market turned south, I saw it as an opportunity to jump in deeper, but the market wouldn't stop turning. Before long my wife and I had lost a small fortune. It was money we couldn't afford to lose at a time in our lives when we couldn't afford to lose it. *If only I had shorted the market, moved into safer stocks, put the money into real estate, hid it all under a mattress.... If only!*

If only we could stop thinking that way, stop dwelling on the past and start living in the moment. If only we could leave our failures in the past where they belong and begin living in the here and now.

KILLING TIME

Henry David Thoreau spoke of "ladies of the land weaving toilet cushions against the last day.... As if you could kill time without injuring eternity."[5] He was writing about being frivolous with our lives and the amount of time we waste doing trivial things with careless attitudes. It's an interesting perspective worthy of thoughtful reflection.

But killing time isn't the only way we injure eternity.

Think of the damage we do to our lives by being fixated on the future, attempting to have a relationship with God based on what we wish we were and wish we had. Why do we think God dwells in our fear, worry, and deferred hope? How often do we injure eternity by being absorbed with things to come?

And what about the past? Think about the ways our relationship with God is obscured by regrets and disappointments. Think of the unwarranted power we give both to the past and to the future. We believe we can kill time in the present moment without injuring our eternal relationship with God.

STEPPING INTO ETERNITY

It is impossible to walk with God in the past or the future; we can walk with him only in the present moment. And because God doesn't submit to a linear time line, every moment is an eternal moment.

Our view of time has led us to think of eternity as something in the future, as some grand blessing to come at the end of this life. But what is eternity if it isn't life with the Eternal One? Eternity is living with God today, being fully alive in his presence moment by moment. Every moment is an eternal moment because every moment can be lived in the company of God.

God longs for us to be fully engaged with him, fully focused on our relationship. He longs for us to step out of our time-limited space and into sacred eternal space. He invites us to step out of ourselves and into eternity with him, to discard the myth of linear time and live in the reality of his immediate presence.

In God's presence you *are enough*. In eternity with God, you *have enough*. In the sacred space, time is always lived in the present moment.

It bears repeating: In this moment, I find God. In this moment, I have all I need.

NINE

At the Age for Love

The Deeper Meaning of Your Defining Moments

Life does not happen to us; it happens from us.
—Mike Wickett

I passed by you again and looked on you;
you were at the age for love.
—Ezekiel 16:8, nrsv

It would be hard to find someone who isn't interested in meeting their soul mate—the person they want to spend the rest of their lives with. It takes most people twenty-five years, many even longer, to find their one true love. But not me (Tim). I found my soul mate early in life, at the age of six. She appeared at the front of my first-grade classroom in the form of my blue-eyed, fair-haired teacher Miss Pond.

The connection between us was undeniable. I'm sure she felt it too. I could tell by the way she spent so much extra time with me, making sure my *A*'s stayed in between the lines and my *C*'s had just enough arch to them. She would often place her hand over mine, gently guiding the pencil along as I wrote. "Very good, Timmy," she'd say, with a knowing sparkle in her eye. "Now try your small letters."

The other kids may have been fooled, but not me. I knew it was true love.

Once she even called me to the front of the class during quiet time when we were all supposed to be reading. She handed me the keys to her car and asked in a whisper, "Can you do me a favor?" She told me she needed a book from her car—a bright red Corvette on the far end of the teacher's parking lot. The book was in a "secret compartment" just beneath the dashboard on the passenger side. "Would you mind getting it for me?" she asked.

"Sure, Miss Pond." I blushed.

A red Corvette. How cool is that? Just like a secret agent on TV! And it had a secret compartment, a place only the two of us knew about. Even more proof that the connection between us was real. We were destined to be together.

At least until I graduated to the second grade. That's when everything fell apart. Now that we were separated by three doors and twenty years, the relationship didn't a chance. I can only hope that Miss Pond was eventually able to move on.

Think about your own story of first love, your first childhood crush. Or perhaps you have a story about simply being in love with love. These feelings tend to pass as quickly as they come because, at the time, you're not yet at the age for love. It is only when you reach the age for love that you can truly give your heart to another.

Just like life, love is a process of growing and maturing, of nurturing and awakening, of coming to terms not just with life but with ourselves and our emotions. And that takes time. The ability to love has to go through seasons, through times of sowing and weeding and fertilizing, through cold nights and blistering days.

And then, when the time is right, love unfolds. We're ready to give our hearts because we're finally at the age for love.

AGAINST ALL ODDS

In ancient times God created a nation to call his own, a people he named Israel. The story of Israel is the life story of a people who are loved by God, protected by God, and nurtured by God. It is the story of a people who often choose to reject the love of God. In many ways, reading Israel's story is like reading our own.

God worked tirelessly to win back Israel's love every time she chose to follow after other gods. It's easy to judge Israel's fickleness, but how different are we? Like you and me, Israel was born naive. Like an infant, she was helpless, unsuspecting, immature. God nurtured and cared for her as he watched and waited for her to develop. Listen to how he described Israel through his prophet Ezekiel:

As for your birth, your umbilical cord wasn't cut on the day you were born, and you weren't washed clean with water. You were not rubbed with salt or wrapped in cloths. No one cared [enough] about you to do even one of these things out of compassion for you. But you were thrown out into the open field because you were despised on the day you were born.

I passed by you and saw you lying in your blood, and I said to you [as you lay] in your blood: Live! Yes, I said to you [as you lay] in your blood: Live! I made you thrive like plants of the field. You grew up and matured and became very beautiful. Your breasts were formed and your hair grew, but you were stark naked.

Then I passed by you and saw you, and you were indeed at the age for love.[1]

Like a baby struggling to grow, Israel lay helpless before the world. As she fought to survive the growing pains of life, struggling through the many stages of infancy, God continued to watch her and nurture her. Time and again he "passed by," waiting for her to reach the age for love. And when he saw that she had matured, he took her in.

So I spread the edge of My garment over you and covered your nakedness. I pledged Myself to you, entered into a covenant with you, and you became Mine.[2]

Israel's growth to maturity was a long and painful process. She endured numerous seasons of sorrow and tragedy, times of rebellion and disillusion, moments of suffering and loss. Like you and me, she wasn't born into awareness; she had to grow into it, to be nurtured into the fullness of life. And only then could God bring her under his covenantal wing.

Because only when we reach the age for love can we fully give our hearts to another.

ONCE BELOW A TIME

In Dylan Thomas's classic poem "Fern Hill," he describes the days of his youth, days of bouncing through apple orchards without a care in the world, of climbing trees and playing in streams and dancing through fields. If you've never read it, you should. It's a poem many of us can relate to.

> Time let me hail and climb
> Golden in the heydays of his eyes,
> And honoured among wagons I was prince of the apple towns
> And once below a time I lordly had the trees and leaves
> Trail with daisies and barley
> Down the rivers of the windfall light.[3]

"Once below a time," wrote Thomas, and we all know instinctively what he meant. There was a time in life before we were even conscious of time. We lived in the here and now, existed only for the moment. It was a time of exuberance and childhood innocence. Life was filled with mystery, wonder, and awe. It was a magical time when the pressures of life had yet to find us, when we had yet to feel the weight of the world on our shoulders. It was a time before we knew that life could be hard and confusing. We all used to live once below a time.

But then we began to grow and to see life differently. Our eyes were opened to the world around us, and our days of laughing and running through apple orchards were fewer and farther apart. We were no longer "honoured among wagons" or "prince of the apple towns"; we were just children walking through a field. The mystery of life began to disappear. Our illusions began to fade. The magic no longer seemed so magical.

Little Timmy learned that Miss Pond's "secret compartment" was no secret at all. It was just a common glove box, just like the one in his dad's old station wagon. Once below a time, life was easy and we were naive. But then we started to grow.

MARKING TIME

One of my (Tim's) earliest and most vivid childhood memories is of a day when I was playing in my father's garage, tinkering with his tools, digging through a jar of nuts and bolts for no particular reason. I think I was about four.

I heard a buzz by the window and looked up to see a small bug, yellow and fuzzy, knocking itself against the pane, trying to escape. I went for a closer look. Over and over the little insect hurled itself at the window, and I tried to figure out why.

I laid my arm across the window ledge and rested my head on it so I could get an even closer view. For the longest time I just stared, my mind slipping in and out of daydreams. Several times the creature brushed against my skin. Once it even landed on my arm, and I sat deathly still so I wouldn't scare it away. Eventually it landed on my forearm, walked up and across my elbow, and then back down toward my hand. It seemed as if it was beginning to trust me. It was a beautiful bug with tiny wings and black stripes across its yellow back, and I studied every move it made.

Then it stopped walking and stood completely still. Suddenly a painful sting shot up my arm. I jumped up and ran and screamed as loudly I could. The little bug was a wasp, and it had stung me for no apparent reason. *Why would it do that?* I couldn't for the life of me understand it.

My mom cleaned the wound, put a bandage over it, and then gave me some medicine to help ease the pain. All the while my confused mind was churning. Before that day, bugs had always been harmless little creatures that were fun to watch and even more fun to play with if you could catch one. But now I knew differently. Some bugs were angry and cunning and cruel.

My painful encounter in the garage changed something in me. I had lost a small measure of innocence. I was no longer as naive and trusting, no longer so gullible, no longer so *childish*. From that moment on, bugs were suspects, not friends. Once below a time, bugs were cute and fascinating. But now they could no longer be trusted.

In his book *The Sacred Journey,* Frederick Buechner writes of his childhood, a time when everything was carefree and innocent and all of life was filled with wonder and hope. Then his father committed suicide and his life shattered. Nothing made much sense anymore. Young Buechner struggled to accept the fact that his father was no longer with them even as he struggled to understand the reason behind his father's actions.

That moment became a mark in time that changed Buechner's life forever. It was a defining moment. He described it as "the first tick of the clock that measures everything into before and after."[4] Everything in his life was measured against this pivotal moment. Now he knew bad things could happen when you least expect them to.

We all have these moments, these time markers that suddenly occur and change our lives forever.

"Tragedy always comes," writes David Crowder. "If it hasn't come for you, it will. Not the losing-your-homework kind or the having-to-flush-your-goldfish kind, but the kind that leaves you stripped. The kind that tears from you all the ideas about living you once believed untearable."[5]

These moments are the ladders we climb one rung at a time to rise from naiveté to awareness. And some steps are far more painful than others.

THE SEEDS OF REGRET

Sharon is a good friend who works as a counselor in a crisis pregnancy center. She has kind eyes and an inviting smile, and every day she counsels young women in trouble. Her clients have made choices they now regret, choices that can only be described as defining moments, time markers. Sharon counsels women who don't need to be reminded of their mistakes; what they need most is a caring counselor like Sharon.

Brittney is a bright and beautiful sixteen-year-old who struggled to find acceptance from her dad. She found it instead in the arms of her first boyfriend. Now she's pregnant, and her father swears he'll never forgive her. He has already kicked one daughter out of the house, so Brittney knows his threats aren't idle ones.

"I'm a good person," Brittney says. "I just made a bad mistake. I know God must hate me."

Rhonda is a junior in high school with dreams of flying jets in the U.S. Air Force. She had her entire future planned until she got pregnant, which jeopardized everything she'd worked for. Abortion seemed to be the only way out, and it was such a simple procedure. But now she can't stop crying. "Nobody told me what it would do to my heart," she says through tears.

Heather, a naive girl from a good Christian family, ended up at the wrong party. She was drugged and raped. Now she's pregnant, confused, and angry—and still waiting for the results of her HIV test. "How can I ever get my life back?" she asks. "It was stolen from me."

These young girls have different stories but one common thread that binds them together. Each of their lives took a turn they never saw coming, and those experiences left them reeling in humiliation and remorse. Each girl is now tagged with a label she never wanted to wear.

Once below a time, life was innocent and easy, and reputations were intact. But now the seeds of shame and regret have been sown.

THE LABEL OF "MEANING"

Is it possible that even these kinds of time markers have meaning in God's economy? Can he use even our deepest, darkest seasons of regret as part of his nurturing process to mature and prepare us for the age for love? Can even the stings we inflict on ourselves have some meaning in God's Story?

We all know that God would never cause us to sin. He would never plant seeds of waywardness into the soil of our lives. But what's to keep him from using our mistakes and failures as tools for nurturing us as he moves us toward the age for love?

The answer depends on which story you're reading. In the human story, the small story, failure and sin lead only to fear, remorse, and shame. We don't attach meaning to these time markers; instead, we label them as guilt, sorrow, or defeat.

But the small story isn't the one that matters. In God's Story, every time marker has only one label, the label of "meaning." In his Story, nothing happens *to* us that he isn't using *for* us.

"In your book were written all the days that were formed for me, when none of them as yet existed."[6] The psalmist embraced the truth that God's care for us existed even before our earthly life began. Not one moment of any of our days has ever gone to waste. All of life is a nurturing process. God uses everything, even our most cross-purposed choices, to create meaning.

"God causes all things to work together for good to those who love God, to those who are called according to His purpose,"[7] wrote the apostle Paul. Every pain and struggle, every disappointment, every time marker in your past is simply another rung in the ladder you are climbing toward spiritual maturity. They all bring meaning and significance to your relationship with God. They all bring you one step closer to the age for love.

THE AGE FOR LOVE

The expression "the age for love" was coined by the prophet Ezekiel, and people have been striving to reach a better understanding of this age ever since. We want to be mature enough, aware enough, and prepared enough to be captured by God's love. But how and when we reach the age for love isn't necessarily what you and I might expect.

Luke wrote about a time when Jesus was eating at the home of Simon the Pharisee. While they dined, a sinful woman brought a flask of fragrant oil and began to anoint Jesus' feet with it. She washed his feet with her tears, wiped off the dirt with her hair, and then kissed them. It was an act of complete humility on the woman's part, and most of us are familiar with Jesus' response: "Her sins, which were many, have been forgiven; hence she has shown great love."[8]

We've all heard the standard interpretation of this story: the woman came to Jesus seeking forgiveness for her sins, and her remorse led Jesus to forgive her. But is that what the passage says? Look carefully at the words: "Her sins, which *were* many, *have been* forgiven, *hence* she has shown great love."

Don't miss the powerful truth in this statement!

Jesus was not describing a woman who had come to him out of remorse and regret for her sins and shamefully knelt at his feet, hoping against hope for a measure of mercy. Some Bible translations have skewed the meaning of this passage by changing the verb tenses. The original Greek gives a clearer picture of the actual meaning of this passage.

Notice Jesus' use of the past tense: "Her sins, which *were* many, *have been* forgiven; *hence* she has shown great love." Something happened to this woman *before* she arrived at Simon's house. We're not told what happened, but clearly her guilt was already behind her. Her sins *were* many and *had already been* forgiven. She came to Jesus not out of guilt or remorse but out of love and gratitude. It was only after she realized how much she had been forgiven that she was able to humble herself and show great love. It wasn't her sinful past that brought her to the age for love; it was her understanding of what God had already done with her past.[9]

The distinction between the two interpretations is critical. The age for love is not something we arrive at simply through the passage of time; it's a state of mind we come to when the reality of God's forgiveness finally hits us. We reach the age for love when we realize the enormity of God's Story and what it does to our story. It's when we understand the depth and breadth of God's grace and what it means for our lives.

While God is nurturing us, he is also waiting for us to reach full maturity, to reach the age for love. Throughout the Old Testament we see God nurturing his people toward the age for love, compelling them to respond not to what he planned to do in the future but to what he had already done for them.

"Return to me, for I *have* redeemed you,"[10] God said through his prophet Isaiah. Israel had been living apart from God, completely disengaged from the relationship, giving her heart to other lovers. Yet God had never turned his back on her. In his eyes, she was already redeemed.

"We love because he first loved us,"[11] wrote the apostle John. We don't find God's acceptance through a life of dogged obedience; we live in obedience because we're already accepted. We love God because he loved us first. We don't love in an attempt to earn his love.

We know we've arrived at the age for love when we finally realize the magnitude of the love and compassion and forgiveness that God has already extended to us. It's also when we finally understand that the Story is not about what we can do but about what God has already done.

And only at the age for love can we truly give our heart to another.

⁓

Once below a time we wondered if God's Story was big enough to cover our most cross-purposed life choices. Now we know that our sin and mistakes and failures have long since been covered. Now we finally understand what it means to be God's own personal concern.

Now we're ready to embrace the Romance...

to open ourselves fully to the Courtship that God has been nurturing...

to accept his proposal of Marriage with eyes wide open.

PART III

A Marriage to Be Consummated

The Power That Binds You

Human things must be known to be loved: but
Divine things must be loved to be known.
—Blaise Pascal

There is a land of the living and a land of the
dead, and the bridge is love.
—Thornton Wilder

It may be said," wrote William Barclay, "that there are two great beginnings in the life of every man who has left his mark upon history. There is the day when he is born into the world; and there is the day when he discovers why he was born into the world."[1]

If we learn anything from the Story of Scripture, we learn that you and I were born for love. We were created *by* Love, *in* Love, *for* Love. We were created for relationship.

In the journey of life, there comes a point in our relationship with God when we reach the age for love. At this point, we cross over from the realm of knowing *about* God into the realm of *knowing* God. We are no longer simply alert in the things of the Story of God; we have become fully aware of their *significance*.

The age for love is the moment when we become intuitively aware of God's pursuit of us. We begin to see that in God's economy, everything has meaning and purpose. Nothing happens *to* us that God isn't using *for* us. We've stepped out of our own small story and into sacred space, God's space. We've entered God's Story.

And in God's Story, we can no longer see things that happen to us as good or bad, abundance or lack, blessing or tragedy, sacred or secular. Everything falls into its rightful place within his cycle of love. It is all part of God's nurturing process, taking us from where we are to even greater vistas of growth.

You and I say it is natural for trees to lose their leaves in the fall; God says it is necessary. Everything we experience is essential in God's divine cycle of love. And in this cycle of love, there is a time to let God complete your relationship, to consummate it by joining your heart to his.

TEN

THE DIVINE PROPOSAL

WILL YOU ACCEPT THE SACRED INVITATION?

The central promise of the Bible is not,
"I will forgive you." The most frequent
promise is "I will be with you."
—JOHN ORTBERG

Who is he who will devote himself
to be close to me?
—JEREMIAH 30:21

Everybody loves a love story. It's written on the pages of our hearts. Whether you're male or female, ten years old or a hundred, a coal miner or a librarian, the minute someone begins telling a love story, your ears perk up. To love and be loved is the most central of all human desires. And we are all, on some level, in love with the idea of love.

Of all the love stories I (Frank) have heard, none have ever quite compared to the story I grew up hearing—the story of my parents, Walter and Veronika. The pretty and petite farm girl from Luxembourg, Germany, and the strapping young GI from Louisiana.

Dad passed on a few years ago, but if I close my eyes, I can still see my parents walking hand in hand down the sidewalk. My mom, barely four feet eleven with jet black hair and a frilly skirt dancing at her ankles, and my dad, a gentle giant of a man at six feet four inches, and even taller with his boots and cowboy hat. They were the most unlikely looking pair you could imagine, but they were as much in love as any two people who have ever walked the planet. Of the many lessons I learned from my parents, one looms above them all: there are true soul mates on earth, and sometimes they find each other.

I grew up in a small house in a small Texas town, and I couldn't begin to count the number of times friends would show up at our doorstep during dinner. They would just "happen" to be in the neighborhood, so they'd stop by. We'd scrunch together and make room for them at the table, and soon small talk would turn to laughing. Then, inevitably, the conversation would come around to the same request: "Mama Martin, tell us the story again."

Mom would smile and reach for Dad's hand. He would blush and make a silly comment like "Don't ask me. I wasn't there" or "I guess you'll have to tell it. I don't even remember getting married." Mom would pretend to push him away, and we'd all laugh. Then in her thick German accent, she'd tell the story.

They met in a small café in France after the Second World War. She was working as a cook for a French colonel, and my dad was one of the many GIs enlisted to rebuild a country that had been torn apart by war. She didn't speak a word of English; he didn't speak a word of German. But that didn't keep them from laughing and flirting with each other across a table crowded with friends. Both of them were shy but were smitten with each other from the first glance.

My mom was horrified when she saw how tall my dad was. "He stood up to walk me home, and he just kept going and going," she'd say with a laugh. "What would my father think?"

She convinced my dad to wait for her outside while she lingered in the café for hours, talking with friends and thinking that he would get the message and leave. When the café closed, she put on her hat and coat to venture home in the rain. When she stepped outside, my dad was still there, still waiting, drenched from head to toe. He just smiled and slipped his raincoat over her shoulders.

"That's when I knew he must really love me," my mom would always say, gently brushing the back of his hair.

"Shoulda run when I had the chance," my dad would say, just to get another laugh.

The story continued on from there and eventually came around to the best part: the day they decided to get married. And this part of the story seldom left a dry eye in the room.

Their courtship was fast and furious even though they couldn't speak each other's languages and could communicate only through smiles and gestures. But my mom had been practicing a phrase in English. It was something she'd wanted to ask her shy American boyfriend.

So one night after dinner, under the light of a streetlamp with raindrops teasing their skin, the two stood face to face, she on her tiptoes on the highest curb she could find, and he with his knees slightly bent. They stood gazing into each other's eyes, communicating the only way they could, through the language of their hearts. Suddenly, in the best English my mom could summon, she asked, slowly, "Do you take me with you to America?"

My dad smiled, fought back a tear, wrapped his long arms around her tiny waist, then pulled her close and kissed her. At that moment they both knew they would be together forever. It was the beginning of a love affair that would span two continents, five kids, and more than fifty years of marital happiness. Dad never found the formal words to propose, nor did he ever need to. They both knew instinctively that it was meant to be.

I've heard the story hundreds of times, and each time it feels as fresh as the first. Each time it brings me one step closer to the power and magnitude of love.

Mom and Dad were led by love. And the world moves for love. It kneels before it in awe.

A METAPHOR OF LOVE

Is it any wonder that God chose marriage as the analogy for describing his relationship with us? Is there another metaphor that could possibly elicit more emotion or give us a better picture of his true feelings for us? Time and again Scripture refers to us as the bride and Jesus, God come in the flesh, as our Bridegroom. The story of Israel is above all the Story of a

Romance and, more specifically, the Story of a Lover in furious pursuit of his beloved. You can't get away from it.

I don't think God is surprised when we have trouble accepting this metaphor. He knows we default to seeing ourselves as unworthy of his pursuit, undeserving of even a minute of his time. I can think of hundreds of reasons that God should reject me, but only a few that might make him want to glance in my direction. Isn't that true for us all?

Maybe that's why God chooses a Romance to make his love real to us. It's lofty and almost too good to believe, but it's also exciting, compelling, and attractive. No one can resist a good romance.

God's Story of divine Romance doesn't make complete sense, but it doesn't need to. It's an image that appeals to our hearts, not our heads. And to push the analogy to the limit, God included in the canon of Scripture the Song of Solomon. It is the most sensual and one of the most challenging books in the Bible. It's filled with images of love and passion, even eroticism. The book describes in vivid detail the longings of a bridegroom for his bride and vice versa. It is, amazingly, a vivid description of God's longings for his people.

The idea that God's love for us borders on sexual longing is so controversial that scholars throughout history have debated whether Solomon's Song should even be included in the canon of Scripture. In fact, the concept of God as a Lover didn't gain general acceptance in Christian circles until the twentieth century.[1] The idea seemed so improper, so risqué even, many refrained from using the metaphor.

But that's exactly how God describes our relationship with him, because he sees it as a marriage, a deep and mysterious joining of both mind and spirit, a consummation of hearts. You and I give ourselves freely and willingly into the arms of God, allowing ourselves to be folded completely into the fury of his love and enraptured by the passions of his desire.

It's the picture of a monogamous relationship, a one-on-one union, an individual marriage between you and God. And by "you" I don't mean the "body of believers"; I mean "you"! You are a beautiful bride in the arms of your helplessly smitten Bridegroom.

Solomon's Song is our private crash course in what it means to be God's own personal concern.

Hearing the Minority Voice

In Scripture, God almost always speaks through the *minority voice*. He does things that don't make sense to the majority, so the majority rejects it. Remember, the apostle Paul said that God uses the foolish of the earth to confound the wise.[2]

The majority voice in first-century Judaism said that the Messiah was supposed to come down in a blaze of glory to set up his Kingdom on earth and that he would rule with the power of a king. But instead, God came down in the form of a helpless baby.

The majority voice, appealing to the Law, said that faithfulness is about rules and regulations, about doing what you're supposed to do when you're supposed to do it and about not doing what you're not supposed to do. But God made it clear that faithfulness is about trust.

The majority voice said that God is the lofty, unreachable Ruler of heaven and earth and that we are nothing but lowly and unworthy slaves. But God came to us in the form of a humble Servant, saying, "Please be mine."

In almost every area of life, God is found somewhere outside the boundaries of the majority voice. We are more often guided to God by the minority voice, and almost nowhere in Scripture does the minority voice cry out with more clarity than in the Song of Solomon.

Look how God describes his feelings toward us:

How beautiful you are, my darling!
Oh, how beautiful!
Your eyes are doves.[3]

Like a lily among thorns
is my darling among the maidens.[4]

Show me your face,
let me hear your voice;
for your voice is sweet,
and your face is lovely.[5]

You are altogether beautiful, my love;
there is no flaw in you.…
You have ravished my heart.[6]

We are not God's causal love interest. His passion screams at us from the pages of Scripture, pleading with us to understand how much we mean to him, how he envisions us in the grand scheme of creation, how earnestly he's working to win our hearts. To borrow a commonly used acronym, we could call the Song of Solomon God's divine SOS call, imploring us to embrace his pursuit and to accept his proposal of marriage.

Like an innocent bride, we stand on the curb, looking up into the eyes of our Lover. We say to him in the best way we know how, "Do you accept me? Will you take me with you to eternity?"

God wipes away a tear and pulls us deep into his loving arms. With his divine kiss he gives us both his heart and his unrelenting love, rapturing us into an incredible and eternal Love Story.

God proposes to us not with the force of a majority voice but with the tender plea of the minority voice: "Come. Let me make you my bride."

So why do we still struggle to see the truth and beauty of God's furious pursuit? Why do we recoil at the idea of God as a hungry, relentless, passion-filled Lover, a starry-eyed Admirer falling to his knees to ask for our hand in marriage? We struggle to see it only because our hearts struggle to accept it. It overwhelms us to think that the Creator of the universe might really love us that much.

And yet that's exactly how much he wants us to be his.

WHEN GOD KNELT DOWN

God on his knees!

Can you imagine the sight? The disciples certainly couldn't.

It was just before the Passover Feast. Jesus knew that the time had come for him to leave this world and go to the Father. Having loved his own who were in the world, he now showed them the full extent of his love.[7]

Jesus was in the Upper Room with his disciples the night before the Passover. For his disciples it was another chance to be with him, to learn from him, to take in a little bit more of his wisdom. But to Jesus it was his final opportunity to show them the full extent of his love. It was his last chance to show his disciples how much they meant to him before the chaos of the Cross would send them scattering in confusion. This was the ideal time and place for an eternal proposal.

> [Jesus] got up from the meal, took off his outer clothing, and
> wrapped a towel around his waist. After that, he poured water into a
> basin and began to wash his disciples' feet, drying them with the
> towel that was wrapped around him.[8]

Jesus used his final evening with his disciples to give them a word picture they would never forget, one that would burn an indelible image into their hearts and minds. He knew that words might soon be forgotten, but a counterintuitive analogy would stay with them for a lifetime. So he grabbed a towel and basin and dropped to his knees in front of them.

He knelt in the posture of a marriage proposal.

It's what any of us would do when we want to make the biggest statement possible to our one true love. When we want to say, "You're the one I want to be with for the rest of my life." When we want to turn a special evening into a monumental memory, we drop to our knees and propose.

Not so long ago I (Frank) was sitting with my family in a crowded restaurant when a sudden hush fell over the room. Something was happening in the far corner, and all over the restaurant people were craning their necks to see. I glanced over and saw a young man on his knees in front of a young woman. The young woman started crying, then she leaned forward to kiss her handsome suitor. At that moment applause broke out across the room. We hadn't heard a word of what was said, yet we all knew we'd just witnessed something special, something binding, something life changing.

Something sacred.

Jesus had a proposal to make, so he began by dropping to his knees.

And what was Jesus proposing? He was asking the disciples to become more than followers, more than the objects of his pursuit. He wanted them to become eternal partners with him, to become one with him for eternity. Not just to join him in his mission or his ministry but to share in his life, his *heart*. To become his bride.

That should have been more than enough. But the proposal went even deeper. In his simple act of humility, Jesus was once and for all settling the debate about who the real Pursuer is and whom he is pursuing. Once and for all he laid to rest any doubts about his commitment to the relationship, his dedication to the eternal pursuit of our hearts. No longer can there be any remaining doubt or suspicion about the depth and breadth of his love for us.

Jesus was saying to his disciples—and to us, "You have ravished my heart! Have I ravished yours?"

Could there be another symbol outside the Cross that is more powerful than our Suitor kneeling in front of us? Could there be any Story in all of Scripture that gives a clearer word picture of God's furious pursuit of us? Could Jesus have done anything else that would have illustrated more powerfully his passion to have us join our lives with his?

When the apostle John wrote, "We love because he first loved us,"[9] he was likely reflecting on this moment with Jesus. It was Jesus who took up the towel and basin, not the disciples. It was Jesus who dropped to his knees before them.

God always takes the initiative in our relationship with him. He pursued us long before we were humanly capable of pursuing him. He is far more invested in this relationship than we will ever be. And his pursuit of us is always more potent, more compelling, more relentless, more *furious* than ours.

THE GOD OF THE TOWEL

Peter recoiled at the thought of Jesus bowing down at his feet. " 'No,' said Peter, 'you shall never wash my feet.' "[10]

He couldn't fathom the concept of God dropping to his knees in front of him, so he instinctively rejected it. He renounced the idea that Jesus would be the One to humble himself and propose. It was so far outside Peter's paradigm that it caused him to raise his voice in anger at Jesus. "No," he snapped, "you will never do that!"

And aren't you and I quick to do the same thing?

The majority voice is screaming at us, "You're not worthy of that! Don't even consider the thought that God would humble himself before you, that he would pursue someone like you, much less propose marriage!" The majority voice tells us that it's up to us to do most of the work in this relationship. It tells us that God is on his throne waiting for us to bow down before him, daring us to draw near, waiting to judge us if we don't. God is at best an elusive target in humanity's quest for an eternal future. God has agreed to draw near, but only if we draw near first. At least those are the messages given by the majority voice.

But the *minority* voice—God's voice—says, "You have ravished my heart! Have I ravished yours?" The minority voice is God reaching for a basin and a towel and dropping to his knees. The minority voice says, "I love you. Will you be my bride?"

The minority voice often gets drowned out by the volume of the majority voice. And what's even more tragic is that the majority voice always sells God short. It always gets the Story of God wrong. It puts God in the smaller story, remakes him in our image, places him in a tightly defined box. The majority voice makes the story about us even though the Story is not about us at all.

Scripture is bookended with the Story of God's furious pursuit, anchored by the Cross, and filled with images of his love and passion. The Song of Solomon clearly displays God's feelings toward us. Jesus himself bowed down in love and humility before us, so how could we possibly come away from it with the idea that God isn't crazy in love with us, pursuing us with all the fury within him? How could we possibly miss it?

We miss it because we've listened to the majority voice, and the majority voice always defaults to the smaller story. If you want to find God, look for him in the minority voice. If you want to see his heart, look for it in the Larger Story. If you want to "catch" God, begin by accepting his divine proposal.

A TABLE FOR TWO

Just over fifty years ago in a small café in France, two starry-eyed lovers sat across a crowded table and noticed nothing but each other. A hundred voices filled the air, dozens of cups and saucers rattled around them, the radio played, the street noise rolled in from outside, but nothing could distract them. Nothing could tear their attention away from each other. The pretty, petite farm girl from Germany and the GI from Louisiana were meant to be together, and on this day they had found each other.

Like the two souls in John Betjeman's classic poem "In a Bath Teashop," they knew nothing but each other:

"Let us not speak, for the love we bear one another—
Let us hold hands and look."

She, such a very ordinary little woman;
He, such a thumping crook;
But both, for a moment, little lower than the angels
In the teashop's ingle-nook.[11]

Years earlier the two might not have noticed each other. They might have sat side by side in this same café but never had a second thought about it. They might have run across their one true soul mate and never known it. But this day they did because they were at the age for love. Life had prepared them for this moment. Love had nurtured them, and their hearts had been waiting for this day even before they had been conceived.

Only when you reach the age for love can you give your heart to another.

A Divine Proposal

You and I are at the age for love, and God has been waiting for this moment. Time and again he has passed by, watching us, nurturing us toward spiritual maturity. Everything in our past has prepared us for this eternal moment in God's presence.

God is kneeling in front of us on one knee, with flowers in one hand and a Ring of Thorns in the other, and an eternal proposal on his lips.

"You have ravished my heart," he says. "Have I ravished yours?"

He's not simply expressing his tender feelings for you; he has already expressed them in more ways than you can count. And he's not looking to extend the Courtship; he's been courting you long enough.

God wants to join your heart to his, to delight in you and have you delight in him forever. He wants deeper access to your heart than you've ever given him.

In this proposal, in this moment, God wants to forever replace the smaller story of your life with his Story. He wants to see you move past your past and live in the present moment with him. He longs to convince you to finally trust him.

"You have ravished my heart," God says.

Has he ravished yours?

ELEVEN

THE TOKEN: A RING OF THORNS

THE SYMBOL THAT SEALS OUR RELATIONSHIP WITH GOD

Many are wowed by his miracles;
few are wooed by his Cross.
—SCOT MCKNIGHT

Nothing in my hand I bring,
simply to thy Cross I cling.
—AUGUSTUS M. TOPLADY

W hen ravished hearts drop to their knees, what follows next is a thing of beauty. A token is given.

And not just any token will do. It must be something of incredible value, something hard won, something that is significant to both parties. The token is a symbol of your promise, a seal of the covenant, a reminder of all that has gone before and all that lies ahead.

When I (Frank) decided to propose to Ruthie, I first searched my heart for a way to show her the depth of my love. I wanted a token, a ring, but not just any ring. It had to be one that meant something.

At that time my prized possession was my Kawasaki motorcycle, a black and silver beauty with a full windjammer and a stereo that piped music into my helmet as I rode. I loved that bike! But Ruthie didn't. She thought motorcycles were dangerous and loud and uncomfortable, so she never rode with me.

Somehow, during my search for the perfect token of love, a near-lunatic thought came to mind. *Maybe I should sell my motorcycle and use the money to buy Ruthie a ring.* In my personal paradigm as a free-spirited road warrior, following through on such a thought was unthinkable. It would be like asking Roy Rogers to shoot Trigger. Like the Lone Ranger leaving Tonto tied to a tree. Some things you just don't do!

Yet I did. I thought about it long and hard and finally decided to make the ultimate sacrifice. I couldn't help myself; I was led by love. And the world moves for love. It kneels before it in awe.

I sold my bike and bought Ruthie a ring. It was the one sacrificial act I could muster to show her the depth and breadth of my love. This token of my commitment would be more than just another piece of jewelry; it would be a lasting symbol of my undying love. It would be a symbol born of sacrifice.

What did the great Romancer do when he wanted to present us with a token of his love and commitment? He made a sacrifice beyond comprehension. A sacrifice so great, so grand, so unfathomable, so "other than" anything you and I could possibly imagine that it left an indelible mark in eternity. He gave us a Ring of Thorns, a crown of ultimate pain and surrender, a token of unarguable love. He presented us with a symbol bathed in blood and born of sacrifice.

The greatest demonstration of love is to lay down our life for another. God could make no greater sacrifice for us. And no token, other than a Ring of Thorns, carries more value and significance.

This crown was more than a symbol of his love; it was an eternal reminder of all that had gone before and all that lay ahead. It was more than his promise to walk with us forever. It sealed a relationship that started at the very beginning in a garden created just for you and me.

It was in this garden that the Courtship first began.

THE GARDEN STORY

You and I began our relationship with God in a perfect garden. You may not remember, but you were there in the mind's eye of God. You were every bit as real to God as Adam and Eve; you were alive in the core of his consciousness. The garden is as much a part of our story as this morning's trip to the supermarket or yesterday's argument with your spouse. It's where our relationship with God finds its roots and where our fellowship with God first went wrong.

The garden is where our cross-purposed tendencies first crossed purposes with our identity as God's own personal concern. Your lips and mine tasted the forbidden fruit.

God placed us in a perfect setting, a place with no cares or trials, no thorns or thistles in sight. A garden more lush and perfect than we could ever have conceived of. And we ruined everything. We rejected intimacy with God and broke off our relationship with him.

God allowed us to stay in his creation, but it wasn't the same. There were problems. Now the day-to-day task of living took effort. Now there were thorns and thistles. We could still bring about new life, still find fruit on the trees and pick raspberries from the bushes, but now we had to navigate thorns in order to do so. The ground now had to be tilled, the trees now needed tending, the weeds now needed thinning, the thorns now had to be dealt with. Life was no longer easy.

Like Adam and Eve, many of us started life in a garden setting—at least a near-garden setting. We all had a small taste of the joy and adventure, the delight and pleasure of the garden—that is, before we grew up and learned that life can be hard and cumbersome.

Gwynne and I (Tim) got married while we were still in college, right before our senior year. It was a great time to get married because everything was so simple. We lived on campus in married-student housing that had some of the nicest rooms available. Our tuition was covered, and our parents were still supporting us, even helping with the cost of our books and our living expenses. We could even eat at the school cafeteria whenever we wanted.

My life went on as it always had. I still played basketball and softball and any other sport I could find, I still hung out in the student center playing Ping-Pong and air hockey, and I still avoided the library at all costs. The only difference was that I now had a beautiful woman living with me, along with all the other perks and privileges that marriage affords. Life was *so* good! Not a thorn in sight.

And then we graduated. We moved to a new city and had to go to work every morning. We started buying our own food and gasoline and started paying rent. When we learned that Gwynne was pregnant with our first child, we realized that we had no medical insurance. The thorns of life were everywhere.

Our garden days were over.

We were still committed to building a future together, to raising kids, to sustaining our marriage, but now we realized the work that had to be done. We had to plant and plow and sweat. We had to navigate the thorns of life.

THE STORY OF THE THORNS

At its core, all of life is the process of bringing about new life—making babies and more babies, tilling the soil so new growth can appear, planting and then pulling to make room for new plants. It's what the seasons of life are all about. Old things die so that new things can take root and grow.

And in every season we're confronted by thorns. We are continually working around things that get in the way. We navigate the thorns of selfishness to build a healthy marriage. We navigate the thorns of laziness to make a living. We navigate the thorns of greed to maintain our integrity. We navigate the thorns of our humanity to sustain and grow our relationship with God.

Yet in the midst of all this, we need to remember that God first placed us in a perfect garden, a place of full and complete fellowship with him, a state of deep and unending relationship. And this is where he wants us.

We're the ones who messed it up. We're the ones who brought about the thorns. And although we are powerless to fix it, God isn't.

God knew that he alone had the ability to bring us back to the garden, but he had to take into account the thorns we had brought forth. And not just the thorns of our humanity but also the thorns of our history, the lost and fractured seasons of our past.

We can see the story of our thorns played out in three macrostories drawn from the history of Israel. Once again, Israel's story is our story.

THE EXODUS STORY

When I (Tim) met Joan, she was in her midforties, but she looked eighty. You could tell she had once been a beautiful woman with fair skin and haunting blue eyes. But Joan's beauty couldn't survive her heroin addiction.

She came to our church because she didn't have anywhere else to turn. Her family and friends had rejected her, and the court system was tired of dealing with her. Joan desperately needed someone to walk with her through the darkness, to be there for her, to encourage her. So she turned to us.

I determined to do what I could to help her navigate the thorns of life. And Joan's thorns were far sharper and more numerous than the thorns we deal with.

Once a week I waited for Joan outside the manufacturing plant where she worked and took her to cash her paycheck. From there I took her to a clinic for her weekly methadone shot that would help wean her off the heroin that was ravaging her body. On the way back to her home, I talked to her, counseled her, made sure she was paying her bills and buying milk instead of drugs. I encouraged her to stay the course, to keep trying, to remain in the struggle no matter what it took.

Joan's life was miserable. It took every ounce of strength she could muster just to get out of bed every morning and go back to the factory, where she worked harder and longer hours than anyone I knew just to get by. Her life was a living hell, but she was determined to beat the drug habit that haunted her. Yet she couldn't do it on her own. She needed someone to be there for her when everyone else had forsaken her.

Like Israel before the exodus out of Egypt, Joan was living in bondage, longing for just a hint of light. She was in chains and needed just a glimmer of hope, a small sign that someday, somehow the dawn would break and she would be free from her slavery. She needed to know that she was not alone in the darkness.

THE EXILE STORY

As a pastor, I (Tim) once taught a divorce-recovery class every Thursday night. People from around the city would come to find healing and acceptance on the heels of broken relationships.

In an effort to reach out to the community, we ran a series of newspaper ads announcing that ours was a church that was all about relationships. We targeted the message directly at those who were hurt and disenfranchised and invited them to a church that would accept them unconditionally. We were serious about our claim, and the people who responded were some of the most wounded people I'd ever encountered.

One Saturday morning during the annual church cleanup day, I was working in the kitchen when a deacon found me and said that a man was outside looking for me.

"Who is he?" I asked.

"He didn't say," the deacon told me. "He just said he wants to meet the pastor who put those ads in the paper."

I headed toward the front hallway and rounded a corner to see the largest mountain of a man I'd ever seen. I'm a big guy myself, about six feet five and 280 pounds, but this man made me look like a jockey. He was huge! I wouldn't even venture to guess his height and weight. Let's just say that he was so massive that the sight of him took me aback. And his face was stern as if he were angry.

"I'm Tim," I said, inching my way toward him with my hand outstretched, hoping he wasn't there to settle some score. "Can I help you?"

"I just wanted to meet the man who said that this is a church that loves divorced people," he said, "because I've never met a church like that."

He told me that his name was Jeff, and we shook hands. I assured him that he was in the right place. I introduced him to a few church members and made small talk for a while. And when I told him how much we'd love to have him join our church family, this mountain of a man started to cry. It wasn't just a few tears either. He started weeping right in front of us. It was the most touching scene you can imagine, this giant who was overwhelmed by the thought that a church would accept him just as he was and embrace him in spite of his broken marriage.

Jeff came to church the next day, and the week after that, and it wasn't long before he had become an integral part of our church family. Along the way we learned that he had played offensive tackle for the Ohio State Buckeyes in the days of Woody Hayes. Yet Jeff was one of the kindest, gentlest souls I'd ever met. One day he asked me if I would baptize him, and I remember thinking, *How am I ever going to get him back up out of the water?* The phrase "buried with Christ"[1] took on new meaning for me that day.

Jeff and I became good friends, and the longer I knew him, the more I appreciated him. In that time I learned about all the Christians and the churches that had rejected him because of his divorce. But our church never rejected Jeff, and because of this, he became one of our most loyal and grateful members. Today he serves on the board of an international outreach ministry, teaching and preaching overseas. We've stayed in touch, and he's doing great things for the Kingdom. But I've never forgotten the first time I met him—the day he broke down and cried in the lobby of our church because he felt utterly alone and unwanted.

Like Israel wandering through the wilderness in search of a home, Jeff was in exile. He was lost and abandoned and dispossessed. His story was the story of a man without a place, a man who had been banished. He was longing to find just a hint of mercy in the wilderness. Jeff needed to know that he was not alone in his exile.

The Priestly Story

James was a teacher of teachers. He ran a school that equipped young ministers to teach people about Jesus. James was as effective and charismatic and interesting as any preacher I (Tim) had ever heard. He had a thick European accent, and he used it to his advantage when speaking. He would slowly articulate his key points in a way that made you hang on every word. Listening to him made me wish I had an accent as well, then maybe I could employ some of the same techniques. He was a fascinating lecturer. And more than that, he was a big-hearted man who loved teaching people about God's love and mercy.

But James had a weakness for women and a wife who was not able to show him physical affection. She suffered from a debilitating disease and spent much of her time in extreme pain. James spent his days teaching and his nights taking care of his wife. He loved her deeply but also longed for companionship. He ended up having an affair, then confessed his sin to the church elders. He told them that he knew how wrong it was and immediately broke off the affair and committed to staying faithful to his wife.

The elders forgave James and reinstated him, and he kept his promise for a time, but once again his weakness got the best of him. He had another affair. This time the elders warned him that they would forgive him once more, but only if it never happened again. "Three strikes and you're out," they told him. Again he assured them that he would stay true to his wife.

A few years later, temptation once again got the best of James. He had his third affair, and the elders made good on their promise. He would no longer be welcome among them. They gave him two options: he could move back to Europe with his wife, or he could stay and be publicly disfellowshiped from the church. James decided to go back to Europe, where he has remained. The problem was solved, at least for everyone but James.

Instead of continuing to walk with him through his problem, James's church decided to cut him off, to send him away. They dealt with sin the same way the priests of Israel dealt with it: stone the sinner and move on. Those in leadership at James's church were more concerned about the reputation of their church than they were about the man who needed help. What could have been a story of victory became just another story of unwelcome thorns. (By "victory" I mean not giving up on James even if it meant walking with him for a lifetime.)

And why couldn't James stay faithful to his wife? Perhaps because he was living in Israel's "priestly" story, a story of rules and regulations but no mercy or grace. It's a story of sin followed by confession and promises to stay faithful, followed by more sin and more confession and more failed promises. It's a pattern that repeats itself over and over but never leads to transformation. It's a story of shame that causes most of us to run and hide because few in the church are willing to invest themselves in helping us negotiate the thorns of our humanity.

James isn't the only one living in Israel's priestly story. In so many ways and in so many places, the church has set up camp on this story. The church often prefers casting out the wrongdoers rather than walking with them through sin to transformation.

THE STORY OF US

These are the stories of our lives.

Some of us live in the exodus story. Like Joan, we live in bondage and darkness, longing for the dawn.

Some of us live in a story of exile. Like Jeff, we're lost and lonely and dispossessed, struggling through the wilderness of life, seeking the promised land of acceptance.

Some of us live in the priestly story. Like James, our lives are defined by repeated patterns of sin, shame, confession, and promises, followed by more sin and shame, followed by even greater promises we know we will eventually break. It is a life with no freedom from guilt, a faith so stuck in religion that it never gets anywhere close to relationship.

Together, these three stories comprise the story of our thorns—the same thorns God had to navigate in order to bring us back into a garden of grace, back into full fellowship with him.

These are the stories we need to let go of, the stories we need to be freed from if we are ever going to find meaningful relationship with God. The stories are so dark, so potent, so steeped in bondage and exile and sin, that only one thing can eclipse them. Only one thing can bridge the gap. Only one sacrificial act demonstrated once and for all the full depth and breadth of God's covenant with us, the full extent of his furious pursuit, the full fury of his love.

Only a Ring of Thorns could do that. Only a symbol of such monumental significance, only a token of ultimate sacrifice and commitment can free the maiden's heart from bondage so she can fully embrace her Divine Pursuer.

So God went to the Cross. He laid down his life. The King stepped down from his throne and into the place of a humble servant in order to bring his bride home.

"MY GOD, MY GOD..."

On the Cross, all the stories of our lives came to one final summit of suffering. All the thorns of life came down on one Man. All the barbs of fear and pain and loneliness, all the stories of exodus and exile and sin, and every brutal thorn that had ever sprouted from Adam and Eve's disobedience—all of them were twisted into one crown of torture and shoved deeply into God's skin as he hung on a tree. All the thorns of shame and rejection and helplessness, all our cross-purposed acts and tendencies, all the weaknesses and frailties of our human condition pierced his flesh.

Can you imagine the weight of it, the burden of it, the shame of it? Can you imagine the sorrow that sliced through Jesus' heart as his mind raced with visions of sin and rejection, as thousands of years of human rebellion coursed through his veins, as he took on the worst part of humanity with the best he had to offer?

"My God, my God, why have you forsaken me?"[2] he cried out as the horrible magnitude of it all bore down on his shoulders. It was the same cry God had heard from the Israelites as they struggled through four hundred years of bondage in Egypt. The same cry as they wandered the desert through forty years of testing, struggling with their sin and inconsistency in their efforts to find God within the boundaries of the Law. It was the cry of Joan as she struggled to overcome her addiction to heroin, the cry of Jeff as he fought to find acceptance, the cry of James as he wrestled with his failure to remain faithful to his wife. It is the cry of every soul in the midst of fear, pain, and loneliness. It is the cry of every person who has ever sought to find God in the smaller story of their lives.

"My God, my God, why have you forsaken me?" Haven't you wondered where God was when you needed him most? Haven't you laid awake at night and cried out to God from the depths of your being, "Where are you? Why have you forsaken me?"

It was that cry that rang through the heart and mind of Jesus as he hung on the cross. And the words didn't come just from *his* depths; they came from yours. It was more than his own pain he was feeling; it was yours. It wasn't his shame he bore; it was yours. It wasn't his bondage and exile and sin that weighed on his heart; it was yours and mine.

"My God, my God, why have you forsaken me?" he cried. But not because he had been forsaken—ultimately, he knew he hadn't been. In that moment he wanted you and me to know that, ultimately, we never will be forsaken either.

FORSAKEN BY GOD?

I (Tim) was no more than seven or eight years old the first time I heard those agonizing words of Jesus. I remember sitting in church with my parents while an older gentleman read Scripture from the pulpit. He was presiding over a Communion service, and he read a passage from Mark about Jesus being crucified. In a deep and reverent tone, he read the entire brutal account, ending with the fateful words, "My God, my God, why hast thou forsaken me?" Then he slowly closed his Bible, leaned close to the microphone, glared solemnly across the room, and said, "Let us pray."

At that moment everything within me was screaming out, "No, let's not! We can't pray now! That can't be how the story ends!" Even as a child I saw the hopelessness and horror in such an ending. *Jesus can't be forsaken, can he? How could that be?*

If God turned his back on Jesus, then what hope do I have? If Jesus, God's only Son, the sinless One, was forsaken by God, then what would keep God from forsaking all of us? What does that say to Joan, to Jeff, to James? What does it say to any of us who have ever cried out in the midst of our pain and loneliness, "I need you, God"?

If God did forsake Jesus, then what is going to happen to me?

It was years before I learned what Jesus meant when he cried out to God in his darkest hour. And it was years before I learned what it means to "invoke" a passage of Scripture.

It was a common Hebrew custom to invoke a passage of Scripture by quoting the first few lines of it. A person would summon the entire passage to mind by speaking the first few words aloud. It was like saying, "A rose by any other name…" or "A penny saved…," and anyone could finish the sentence.

That's what Jesus was doing. As he cried out from the depths of his humanity, he summoned the strength to invoke the faithful promises of God. He quoted a well-known passage from one of David's psalms. And by quoting the first few lines, he was invoking the entire passage. Many of us miss it, just as some at the foot of the Cross may have.

My God, my God, why have you forsaken me?
> Why are you so far from saving me,
>> so far from the words of my groaning?…
All who see me mock me;
> they hurl insults, shaking their heads:
"He trusts in the LORD;

let the LORD rescue him.".…

A band of evil men has encircled me,

they have pierced my hands and my feet.…

They divide my garments among them

and cast lots for my clothing.[3]

These messianic words of David foretold Jesus' death a thousand years before his birth. And it happened just as the psalm described. But the psalm didn't end there. You can't stop until you get to the most potent part, the words I longed to hear when I was a boy sitting in church during Communion. These are the words we all need to hear:

For he has not despised or disdained

the suffering of the afflicted one;

he has not hidden his face from him

but has listened to his cry for help.[4]

These words frame the master portrait of Christ's gift. They bring clarity and understanding to Jesus' cry. He wasn't forsaken by God. He knew that God could not turn his back.

His cry was not a cry of defeat; it was a shout of victory! Jesus stepped into the pit of darkness and seized hold of the dawn unfolding before him. He stepped into despair and believed in love. He walked through the valley of the shadow of death and bore our fears because God was with him. God was waiting to walk with him through the darkness, to take him by the hand and deliver him from evil.

Jesus was never forsaken. No one has ever been forsaken by God. And no one ever will be. We may doubt this. It may even seem counterintuitive based upon what we've experienced. So read on…

HE HAS DONE IT!

God has not hidden his face.

That's what Jesus was trying to tell us as he cried out from the Cross. That's the message he wanted you and me to hear. And we haven't even reached the end of the psalm. The best part is yet to come.

> Future generations will be told about the Lord.
> They will proclaim his righteousness
> > to a people yet unborn—
> > *for he has done it.*[5]

Even *in* death Jesus was saved *from* death.[6] God walked with Jesus through the darkness, and because of that, death didn't get the last word. God stayed with Jesus until the end, and because he did, the Story ended exactly as it was supposed to. On the Cross, God navigated the final Ring of Thorns—the most brutal thorns of all—and won.

Think about the meaning this brings to God's token of ultimate sacrifice. Think about what it says to those who feel forsaken by God.

Think of what the Ring of Thorns says to the Joans of the world: "If you're in bondage, struggling through addiction or helplessness, fighting your way through the darkness, you are not alone. There is dawn at the end of the night. God has not forsaken you!"

Think of what it says to the Jeffs of the world: "When you feel alone and powerless, discarded by a world that doesn't want you, fighting your way through the wilderness, God is right beside you. He will always be with you. He never turns away!"

Think of what it says to James and others like him: "Your past is forgotten, your part in nailing Jesus to the Cross, your life of sin and rebellion and inconsistency are completely forgiven. God's Story is bigger than yours. The Cross is big enough to carry your darkest sin. The thorns of your life have already been navigated, for he has done it!"

To every one of us, the Ring of Thorns says, "Even *in* death you will be delivered *from* death because Love always gets the last word!"

Through the Ring of Thorns, Jesus openly confirmed the Story of God once and for all by sealing his covenant with us. God navigated thousands of years of thorns, thousands of years of rebellion, thousands of years of bondage and exile and sin, and thousands of years of darkness to finally bring us back to the garden, back into full fellowship with him. Our relationship with God is sealed forever, for he has done it.

The work is complete. The Story of God is fulfilled. God is on his knee with a dozen roses in one hand and a token of his unending love in the other. And all he's waiting for is you.

Long before the Gift of Christ, God promised Joshua, "I will never leave you nor forsake you."[7] Are those of us living on this side of the Cross to believe that God's promise to us is anything *less?* If anything, his promise to us is even more certain. And God always keeps his promises.

Always!

And this is only *one* of the eternal promises the King makes to his beloved.

TWELVE

THE VOWS OF A SACRED LOVER

WHAT GOD DOES TO RESTORE YOUR HOPE

The supreme happiness of life is
the conviction that we are loved.
—VICTOR HUGO

The LORD is faithful to all his promises
and loving toward all he has made....
You open your hand
and satisfy the desires of every living thing.
—PSALM 145:13, 16

When I (Tim) counsel couples who want to get married, I always ask if they've taken time to write out their wedding vows. I'm not asking for anything elaborate; just a few words they will exchange during the ceremony. Typically they stop gazing into each other's eyes just long enough to turn and give me a puzzled look.

"Oh yeah," they say. "I guess we need to do that."

Then after a few minutes of contemplation, with wrinkled foreheads and sober expressions, they say, "We can't think of anything."

They are thrilled when I help them write some vows—or give them some standard lines to use—because then they're free to go back to gazing into each other's eyes.

To young couples in love, vows are often an afterthought—just something else they have to dispense with to get to the best part of the wedding. And I never get used to that. It's like sprinkling diamonds on your child's Froot Loops and then watching as he picks them out and piles them to one side so he can enjoy the cereal.

I've presided over more weddings than I can count, yet in all my time as a pastor, I've yet to hear a young couple say, "What I'm really looking forward to is exchanging vows."

I've seen people completely obsess over the freshness of the flowers or the placement of the cake or the color of the ribbons. I've seen brides fall apart because a caterer delivered the wrong flavor of mints, but I've rarely seen a couple stress over the vows. It's the most critical part of the ceremony, yet most couples see it as just something else they have to do.

Who put all these rocks in my Froot Loops?

I understand because that was me. When Gwynne and I got married, I was far more eager to get to the reception than to endure the wedding ceremony. I was determined to have the most fun postwedding party that had ever been thrown—and I did! Who needs those little bell-shaped mints and cucumber sandwiches? We had *real* snacks—like big bowls of cashews and peanut M&M'S and Fannie May mints imported from Chicago—along with every flavor of soda pop you can think of, including the kind with twice the caffeine. It was a party to beat all parties. One hundred-year-old men were so hopped up on sugar, they couldn't quit dancing! (Okay, maybe not.) But to this day I couldn't recite all of my wedding vows. My dad performed the ceremony and had a "standard" set that we deemed good enough.

That's how it is. Marriage vows are often seen as just another ritual. That's why so many couples put little thought into writing them. Then again, maybe that's not it. Maybe it's because they've put so little thought into *keeping* them. It's not really their fault. They just haven't lived long enough to see the significance of the covenantal relationship between husband and wife.

Think about married couples who choose to renew their vows. When couples come to me after ten, twenty, or thirty years of marriage and say they want to restate their vows, it's a completely different story. The vows suddenly become the most important part of the evening. They spend weeks honing them; they spend countless hours wording then rewording their thoughts. They want their vows to be perfect, to make a statement, to mean *something special.*

Most of these couples can't remember what they said the first time around, but now, after years of getting to know each other, of making and breaking commitments, they obsess over what they're going to say when they reaffirm their love. They want every word to count. They've seen enough broken promises to know the importance of a promise kept. So they word their vows carefully and state them with intention.

Isn't this how it is with God? Who has seen more broken promises than he has? Who has suffered through more broken covenants and forgotten commitments than he has? More than anyone else, God understands the importance of a vow, the significance of a promise kept. When God makes a vow, you can be sure he chooses his words carefully and states them with complete resolve. God doesn't make promises unless he intends to keep them.

HOUSES ON SAND OR STONE?

Jesus told a parable about two men. One was a wise man who built his house on a foundation of stone; the other was a foolish man who built his house on sand. Then a combination of rain, wind, and a rising tide washed away one of the houses. The house built on sand "fell with a great crash."[1]

You could walk into any Sunday-school class and ask which house withstood the storm, and every person in the room would answer correctly—even the three-year-olds. In fact, that's a great thing about the stories Jesus told: they're easy to remember and even easier to relate to. We've been to the beach and seen the sand wash away with the tide. We've written our name in the sand only to see the first wave erase it. We've seen television news footage of million-dollar homes falling off the eroding cliffs of the Pacific Coast. Everybody knows what happens when you build a house on the sand.

But that's not the point of the parable. Jesus wasn't giving practical advice to homeowners. The real story is about you and me, about what we put our faith in, about whom we lean on in times of trouble. The rains and the winds and the rising of the tide—well, that's just life happening. Life is hard, and sometimes it really starts to beat against us. Whether we stand or collapse depends on what—or whom—we've chosen to lean on. Jesus wants us to understand the difference between building a life on sand and building it on stone.

Ask any group in any church, "Who should you lean on when times get tough: God or people?" and they won't hesitate before answering, "God, of course."

My wife used to teach a class full of two-year-olds, and no matter what question she'd ask, they would always give the same answer: "God and Jesus." They were right about 70 percent of the time. Even when they were wrong, they still got a cookie, because at least they got the ultimate point of the lesson.

We all know the right answers when we're sitting in a religious setting. So why do we miss the point in real life? We have no doubt about whom we can depend on in times of trouble, yet when trouble comes, we tend to rely on the most *undependable* sources available—ourselves and other people. We seek support from those who are the least stable, those who have broken promises in the past, those who have let us down and are just as weak and unreliable as we are. We build our houses on mountains of sand.

Meanwhile, God has never let us down. He has never broken a promise and has never given us reason to doubt him. So why, when we are in trouble, do we prefer to build our lives on sand?

SANDCASTLES OF WORTH-*LESS*-NESS

"Everybody is somebody else's weirdo." When I (Tim) make this statement in front of an audience, people laugh because they can relate. We're all twisted and strange in our own special ways, and we all know at least one person who's slightly more twisted and strange than we are. It's what keeps life interesting.

It's also what keeps us comparing ourselves to others. We're all worried about looking strange, so we're constantly on the lookout for someone who is even stranger than we are. It's self-assuring to be able to say, "At least I'm not *that* guy!"

When I was growing up, I had an aunt who made Cruella De Vil look like Mary Poppins. I hated it when she came to visit because she always made me feel like an idiot. "Tim, can you name all the books of the Bible? Joey can. Joey, name all the books of the Bible for Tim, then we'll see if he can do it." Or "Tim, can you name all the apostles? Sue can, can't you Sue? I'll bet Tim doesn't know them all."

It seemed like my aunt's entire visit revolved around making me feel inferior to her kids. I felt like a heretic standing in front of the Inquisition. I was always on the defensive because I didn't know the answers like her kids did.

In our family, knowing the Bible was everything. And I mean the *entire* Bible—from the introduction to the index, including the maps and time lines. My family comes from a long line of preachers and church elders, all the way back to Pentecost. I often joke that if you're just a deacon in my family, you don't even get invited to the reunions. I grew up convinced that there were degrees of salvation—a graduated scale based on how much Scripture you knew—and I was just barely hanging on. And if I ever forgot how stupid I was, Aunt Cruella was there to remind me.

As if that weren't enough childhood trauma, I was the most math-challenged person on the planet. I did okay until I got to advanced calculations—like subtraction. I got lost about four months into the first grade, and I never caught up.

I spent my school years avoiding math, always taking the easiest courses I could find, always just squeaking by. And then, in college, I decided to major in business. No one bothered to tell me that math is an important aspect of business, but I found out when I took a class called Quantitative

Business Analysis. It just now took me twelve attempts and the help of Microsoft's online dictionary to spell the name, so I'm not sure what made me think I could pass the course. Day after day I sat watching the teacher run together all manner of letters, numbers, and symbols on the chalkboard. I took detailed notes that I was no more successful at understanding than I was at spelling Quantitative Business Analysis. Once again I was the stupidest person in the class.

I'll never forget the first test we had to take. The teacher said it would be easy—just a review of basic algebra—so we shouldn't even have to study for it. That was good enough for me, so I took him at his word and didn't study. The day we got our tests back, I heard grumbling all around the room. "Ninety-four? What did I miss?" "Ninety-six? I thought I got them all right!"

Then came my test. I got a six. I couldn't believe it. "You mean I got one right? Yes!"

When it comes to math, I am diagonally parked in a parallel universe.

We all have something in our past that makes us feel that way. Not necessarily worthless, just worth *less* than others. There is always something that makes us feel stupid, separate from everyone else.

We've all built sandcastles of worth-*less*-ness. *We* erect our self-image on the shifting soil of comparison. We define our worth in relation to others and then wonder why we feel that we're worth *less* than the person next to us.

And this isn't the only castle we build in the sand.

Sandcastles of Ugliness

Feeling stupid or incompetent is tough, but at least you can hide it most of the time. You can pretend that you're bright and witty, that you're just like everyone else. And if you get caught being stupid, you can pretend that you're just pretending to be incompetent. But what do you do when you feel ugly, when you're certain that others are repulsed by the sight of you?

When I (Frank) was a teenager, I had more pimples than any person I'd ever known. I woke up one morning at the age of fourteen with one zit on the end of my nose, and it multiplied from there until zits took over completely. I couldn't do a thing about it. By the time I was sixteen, I felt hideous, like a freak of nature, like a creature that belonged in a bell tower.

It didn't help that I worked in a bakery, standing over a doughnut fryer several hours a day with grease steaming into the pores of my skin. It was my own private pimple factory. No amount of acne medication could stand up to the marauding hordes.

My kids tease me about my high-school photos because I had thick bushy hair that surrounded most of my face. I tell them it was the sixties, but in reality the haircut was my attempt to cover up the zits on my forehead and cheeks. I developed insecurities during those years that still haunt me. The scars of inferiority and the wounds of rejection don't easily go away.

It's easy to look back and laugh at ourselves, but we all know there is nothing funny about feeling discarded. Feeling worth-*less* is nothing to snicker at. It hurts to be rejected, unattractive, mediocre. It's painful to feel like you're in a circle all by yourself. And we've all felt that way. The sandcastles of ugliness find a place to reside inside each of us. Whether you were a homecoming queen or an ogre, you've allowed someone to make you feel inferior at some point, and the lesions are no doubt still with you.

And this isn't even the most heartbreaking castle we build in the sand.

SANDCASTLES OF THE FORGOTTEN

What would a child be without a hero?

First, he wouldn't be normal, because we all have at least one hero in our lives. At some point we look outside ourselves to discover what we want to become. And we identify a hero, a role model, someone we can look up to.

At the age of twelve, I (Tim) had the greatest hero of all: Larry. He was the coolest man on the planet, hands down. Larry was a youth minister at a church in a nearby city. He was good looking, fresh out of college, and adored by everyone who knew him. He was also muscular and athletic, with a golden smile and an even more golden tan. When he spoke, he could mesmerize an audience. Larry was the most flawless human being I'd ever met. Like Batman, Superman, Spider-Man, and the Fantastic Four all rolled into one. Larry was the ultimate *hero*.

And the most amazing thing about him was that he wanted to spend time with me. When I was a junior-high student, he came to stay at our house during a summer youth retreat, and he included me in all the high-school functions. He introduced me to his friends and treated me like I was someone special. I'd spent most of my life feeling like an outsider—like the biggest loser on the playground—but Larry treated me like one of his best buddies. I got to be with him all day every day. I thought I'd died and gone to heaven.

Larry was a champion handball player, and one day he loaned me one of his gloves and taught me how to play. He and I played for hours, hitting the ball against the back wall of our church building. Just two buddies hanging out and having fun. All these years later, I still wonder why a guy like Larry would want to spend time with someone like me. It's amazing how deeply ingrained our insecurities become.

One day during the youth retreat, Larry said, "Hey, Tim. At the end of the summer, I'm taking the high-school youth group up to Kings Island for the weekend. The problem is, my wife doesn't like roller coasters or water rides, so I'll be all by myself a lot of the time. If I swung by and picked you up, do you think you'd be able to go with me?"

"That'd be fun!" I told him, trying to sound cool.

"Great," he said. "Put it on your calendar and make sure you pack enough for the whole weekend, 'cause it's gonna be a long trip."

For the next half hour, he talked about all the fun we were going to have. We were going to hit every ride in the park and stuff ourselves with popcorn and cotton candy. It was going to be the greatest day of my life! Like I'd won the "fun lottery."

I'm sure my parents got sick of hearing me talk about it, but it was all I could think about for the next two months. The night before Larry was supposed to pick me up, I had my bags packed and sitting by the front door. I lay awake all night imagining the fun we were going to have. I even got up a couple of times to check my backpack just to make sure I hadn't forgotten anything.

I was up at six the next morning, sitting on the front steps with my bags piled beside me. Larry hadn't said what time he was coming. He'd just said to be ready, and I didn't want to miss him. So I waited.

And waited.

And waited…

Several times my mom came out and sat beside me. "Are you sure you have the right day?" she asked.

"Yeah, he's just running a little late. He'll be here in a minute," I said, trying not to sound worried. But the longer I waited, the more my heart sank.

Morning turned to afternoon, afternoon turned to evening, evening turned to nightfall, and still no sign of Larry. But I just knew he would come, so I didn't give up.

At ten that evening my mom came out onto the porch and put her hand on my shoulder. "Tim, I'm sorry. I really think you should come in now. Larry must have forgotten you."

Someone could have ripped my heart out through my throat and it wouldn't have hurt any worse. I was absolutely devastated. I dragged my bags back into the house, through the den, and into my room. Then I slipped underneath the covers and cried myself to sleep. I'd never felt so unwanted in my life.

That moment became an emotional time marker, a pivotal point in the time line of my existence. Even today I feel sorrow when someone breaks an appointment with me. It could be something as simple as a date for lunch or a meeting over coffee, but if the plans fall through or someone calls to cancel, it takes me immediately back to the day I waited and waited for Larry to show up. A reminder of that pain and rejection comes flooding back at the smallest hint of disappointment.

Is there any pain in life greater than the pain of being forgotten, feeling that you're so small and insignificant to others that you're nothing more than an afterthought? When someone you care for overlooks you, all your self-doubt and insecurities rush to the surface, and you are convinced of your worth-*less* status.

THE WAY OF TRUST

The details of our stories may vary, but not the themes. To some degree we all feel worth-*less* and ugly and forgotten. We all struggle with deep-seated insecurities because of the power we give to others. We build on sand only to have it shift and erode beneath our feet. We watch helplessly as our lives come crashing down when we're hit with the rain and the wind and the rising tide.

Maybe that's why we struggle to trust God. Our lives are so damaged by broken promises that we've lost the ability to hope. "Who needs a heart when a heart can be broken?" belts out Tina Turner,[2] and we've all set our jaws in agreement. More than anything we want to feel confident about our relationship with God. We want to believe that he's crazy about us, that our greatest Hero truly does want to be our best friend. We want to hope in God, to trust in his love. But we can't hope because we're so afraid he'll forget about us. We fear we'll discover that he's given us just a bunch of empty promises.

We imagine ourselves sitting on the front porch of our dreams as the darkness invades what once was a morning of hope. So we protect our hearts. We keep God at arm's length. He whispers his promises into the depths of our spirit, yet we shut him off. It's a struggle to believe what he's saying, to put our faith in him, to lean on him in times of trouble, to build our lives on the stone of his eternal vows.

In the wreckage of crushed dreams and broken promises, what would it take to convince us that God can be trusted, that he is faithful to his vows? How can we know in our souls that he will never leave us, never break a promise? The doubt and fear are understandable, and the answer continues to elude us.

Perhaps it's as simple as placing your hand into his, lifting your eyes to meet his longing gaze, and saying, "I do. I do trust you. I trust your promises. I accept your proposal. I give you my life, my future, my hopes, my dreams."

Perhaps that's the real secret to finally engaging with God in this eternal courtship, the first step in joining your heart to his once and for all. Trust is the one thing that frees you finally to surrender yourself completely to his love. You have to simply give in. You have to *decide* to trust him.

"I have never had clarity," Mother Teresa once said. "What I have always had is trust."

The way to trust is nothing more and nothing less than this: place your hand into God's and surrender.

⁓

Now that you, the object of God's furious pursuit, have reached the age for love, there are some things your Bridegroom wants you to hear. Listen closely to these sacred vows from his heart to yours:

1. I have always been there for you, and I always will be. I was there when life was simple and carefree, before you knew the pain, loneliness, and isolation of taking responsibility for your choices and then suffering the consequences. I was there through the years you wallowed in immaturity. I came by again and again, nurturing you and waiting for you to reach the age for love.

I was with you in the garden when your lips first touched the forbidden fruit, when your humanity first crossed purposes with my perfect plan for you. I was near when you discovered how unfaithful, inconsistent, and unlovable you could be.

I was there when you gave your heart to other lovers, when you traveled to faraway lands and prostituted yourself and lived with pigs. I was also there when you returned, eager to slip the ring of kinship onto your finger.

I have always been there for you, and I always will be.

2. I will walk with you forever—just the two of us. In this eternal moment, you are enough and you have enough. You have complete access to me every minute of every day. I long to walk with you in the present, to fully engage with you in relationship. I long to hear you say, "In this moment, I find God. In this moment, I have all I need."

Even when your heart and mind are miles away, I will always be right beside you, courting you, whispering in your ear, "I'm right here." I vow to walk with you forever. I will never forsake you. When all others reject you, I will be there with you. I know the pain of rejection. I've suffered the loneliness of exile. I've struggled through temptation, and I've endured the unfaithfulness of others. I've navigated the story of your thorns and even felt the sting as they pierced my skin, but I stayed the course. I remained faithful to the end. And I will remain faithful to you.

3. I will always understand you. Others may know what you've done, and they may define you by things they've seen in your life, but I *understand* you. I understand your pain, your loneliness, your humanity. I understand your heart. I've seen your darkest thoughts and actions, yet I love you deeply. There is no sin of yours that I choose to see, no transgression that the Cross doesn't cover. When I look at you, I see only love. I alone understand you, and I always will.

4. I will always be kind to you. Others will hurt you, but I never will. Others will make you feel awkward and ugly and unwanted, but I will always be kind to you. I will never leave you on the porch waiting and wondering. I will never forget you or leave you behind. I will never make you feel worth-*less*. I vow to always be kind to you.

5. You will always be my own personal concern. Every time you sink into the small story of your life, I will be there to lift you back into the Larger Story. Every time you begin to feel like nothing more than a lowly child, I will be there to remind you of your true identity. Every time you run, I will chase you. I'll pursue you to the bottom of the ocean or the end of your iniquity. I will never let you go, never stop loving you. I will *never* give up on you. You were made *in* Love, *by* Love, *for* Love. You are now and will always be my own personal concern.

6. I love you. I always have, and I always will. Wherever you turn, I will find you. Wherever you go, I will be there to bring you home. No matter how far you stray, how hard you fight to get away, I will never leave your side, never be distant or indifferent. Nothing will ever keep you from my loving arms. "Neither death nor life, neither angels nor demons, neither the present nor the future, nor any powers, neither height nor depth, nor anything else in all creation"[3] can separate you from my love. I vow to love you forever.

Those are the eternal vows of a sacred Lover, vows that will never be compromised or broken. Your heart and mind may fight them, but they can never diminish them. And you can never escape them. Wherever you go, whatever you do, God will find you. Love will find you.

The words of a beautiful ballad written by Nichole Nordeman say it all: "He's right behind you now; just turn around."[4]

HE'S NEVER FAILED ME YET

Just over thirty years ago, at a train station in London, a group of young filmmakers came across a band of transients. The film crew was making a documentary about people who were living on the streets and made their homes in abandoned rail cars and makeshift shelters.

As a group of transients was being filmed, several of them began singing various songs, drinking and hamming it up for the cameras. The filmmakers obliged them.

Then one of the filmmakers, a young man named Gavin, noticed an older man sitting off by himself. He wasn't drunk, and he wasn't really part of the group. He was just a lone transient warming himself at an open fire. He was unshaven and looked far older than his years. He, too, seemed to be singing, but only to himself. Gavin couldn't make out the words of the song, so he moved closer and aimed a microphone in the man's direction. As the man sang, Gavin still couldn't make out the words.

Back at the sound studio, while editing the film and tape, Gavin came across the recording of the lone transient. Gavin turned up the volume and listened. He could barely make out the words. It was a tune he'd never heard, and it had only a few lines of lyrics that the man kept singing over and over:

Jesus' blood never failed me yet,
Never failed me yet, never failed me yet.
This one thing I know, for he loves me so.[5]

The man sang in an almost childlike voice, a hopeful voice, and he could barely carry a tune. But Gavin was fascinated. He wondered what might happen if he recorded some music behind the man's song. He improvised a simple piano accompaniment, then dropped in some digital strings and drums. When he had what he wanted, he started looping the tune, changing it each time in order to give the music greater depth. At one point he decided to let the computer do the work and went to get a cup of coffee, leaving the door to his studio open.

Gavin's studio was in a small room next to a busy art gallery with people constantly coming and going. He was only gone for about twenty minutes, but when he returned, he noticed that the art gallery was unusually quiet. No customers were milling about; there was just a group of people huddled outside the door of Gavin's studio. Some of them were weeping.

All that could be heard was the sound of the lone transient's voice, his tender words repeated over and over. "Jesus' blood never failed me yet. Never failed me yet, never failed me yet. This one thing I know, for he loves me so."

The simple lyrics moved the people to silence. The transient had struggled through more pain than most of us ever will. At his darkest moment, he reached out to the only One he knew was still there. The only One who had never left his side. God had never abandoned him, and those who overheard his simple words of trust and hope were overcome with emotion.

The man's words resonate because they are words we all want to believe. They are words we all long to hear. The blood of Jesus is a simple, powerful, eternal vow of love that we all need to trust.

"Jesus' blood never failed me yet. Never failed me yet, never failed me yet. This one thing I know, for he loves me so."

THIRTEEN

THE VEIL IS LIFTED

THE TRANSFORMING LOVE OF GOD DOES ITS WORK

What lies behind us and what lies before us are tiny
matters compared to what lies within us.
—OLIVER WENDELL HOLMES

Every creature seeks its perfection in another.
—MARTIN LUTHER

It's nearly impossible to turn on your television without running across another reality-TV program, each one more contrived than the last. It's nothing new, really. I've been watching reality TV since I was a kid. It's called football. It doesn't get any more real than that!

I'm not a big fan of the new reality shows, but one of them did catch my eye. It was an extreme-makeover program in which an engaged couple received brand-new looks before their wedding. At the start, the lovers were a plain-looking young couple, sweet people, but not visually perfect. They were a bit overweight with drooping chins and crooked teeth and flabby waists. And they were absolutely crazy about each other.

The couple agreed to work with a team of makeover specialists for several months before their wedding; and they had to remain apart the entire time. They wouldn't see each other again until she was walking down the aisle.

They underwent numerous surgeries and maintained a demanding exercise regimen. Their noses and teeth were straightened, their jaws were moved forward, implants were implanted, and fat was removed—some of it was even put back into different parts of their bodies. Several times they broke down and cried, pleading for the reconstruction to stop. But then they'd buck up and start another round of surgeries and exercise and dental work.

Eventually it all came together just in time for the show's grand finale—their wedding day.

I'm a bit embarrassed to admit it, but at the thought of their reunion, I cried like a little girl as the hourlong show built to its climax. The young bride and groom were waiting to see each other again for the very first time since the makeover.

The veiled bride got the first glimpse as she walked down the aisle toward her nervous groom. He was handsome and rugged looking, with a strong jaw line and chiseled physique. He was nothing like the sweet ugly duckling who had won her heart. She reached underneath her veil to wipe away a tear.

Then as she stood facing her handsome prince, you could see his hands shake as he slowly lifted the veil to reveal his bride. Her skin was soft and tan, her teeth were perfect and white, her figure was now thin and shapely. His once plain and insecure maiden had been transformed into a stunningly beautiful princess.

The two stood face to face in complete wonder and excitement at the sight of each other. Tears streamed down their cheeks as they gazed into each other's eyes. Here were two people who had lived their entire lives feeling inadequate. Their doubts and insecurities ran deep. But today they felt special. Desirable. *Perfect.*

At this moment, they were everything they had ever longed to be. And in many ways, it was a glorious thing to witness.

GOD'S EXTREME MAKEOVER

We all dream of getting our own extreme makeover. We long for the day when we will be special, desirable, perfect. And we don't seek just a physical makeover; we want to be transformed spiritually. We long for an *inner* transformation.

Physical improvement is nice, but how long can it last? As good as this young couple looked standing at the altar, we all know what will happen. Give them ten or twenty years, and once again their hips will sag and their chins will droop and their skin will start to wrinkle. Outward transformations are only temporary. It's the inward kind that makes a greater mark. And it's inward transformation that God promises.

"And we, who with unveiled faces all reflect the Lord's glory," wrote the apostle Paul, "are being transformed into his likeness with ever-increasing glory, which comes from the Lord."[1] It's a promise we've heard often, but it's easy to miss. We hear it, yet we never quite claim it. We see the *things* in the promise of God, but not the *significance* of those things.

"You and I are the product of an extreme makeover," Paul is telling us. "This is a transformation of the highest order—an *inner* transformation." We are *new* creations, beautiful and flawless, perfected through the blood of Jesus. This change is eternal. It's an extreme makeover of the heart and soul. And we have it *now.*

The makeover began with Abram on the day he slept while God walked alone between the severed pieces of the animals, confirming his covenant with Abram by his own name[2] "since there was no one greater for him to swear by."[3] The makeover surgery began at that moment as God promised to fix our flaws once and for all. Our blemishes were too numerous to count, our inadequacies too overwhelming for us to bear. God promised to restore us to full beauty, pledging to fix the ugliness that permeated our lives. The makeover reached a climax through Jesus' work on the Cross, when a new covenant was ushered into the world—a new day of freedom, hope, and splendor.

Prior to the surgery of God's extreme makeover, our lives were filled with shame, doubt, and death. The old Law exposed the depths of our ugliness, producing guilt and condemnation. But the new covenant, God's extreme makeover through the glory of the Cross, changed all that. It took time, pain, and patience on God's part, culminating some two thousand years ago in the most gripping grand finale in all of history.

For if the ministry of condemnation had glory, the ministry of right-eousness exceeds much more in glory. For even what was made glori-ous had no glory in this respect, because of the glory that excels. For if what is passing away was glorious, *what remains is much more glorious!*[4]

No longer do we exist within the smaller story of our sin and faith-*less*-ness. That's the part of us that passed away when God made us new cre-ations and lifted the veil to reveal his beautiful bride. Gone are the guilt and shame and remorse. After God works his makeover, any insecurity we feel is imagined because in God's eyes we are perfect.

LIVING IN THE LARGER STORY

Still, we struggle to accept our new identity. We struggle to feel beautiful in God's eyes. We continue to fight the pangs of guilt and doubt. We insist on holding on to our smaller stories even though God tells us they no longer exist to him and that now we exist only in his Larger Story.

Like Joan, who was struggling to overcome heroin addiction, we are searching for a hint of light at the end of a long, dark tunnel. But God says there is no more darkness, no more shame.

Like Jeff, who had been banished from Christian circles after his divorce, we seek mercy in the wilderness. But God promises that even in the wilderness, he is there with us.

Like James, who failed again and again in his attempts to be faithful to his wife, we fight to overcome habitual sin. But God says we are new cre-ations. In his Larger Story our sins are forgotten.

In the Larger Story there are no chains of bondage, only love and freedom.

In the Larger Story there is no exile, no distance between us and God.

In the Larger Story our sins are no longer visible to God.

In the Larger Story Love has found you. And he will never let you go.

In the Larger Story Jesus' blood will never fail you.

In the Larger Story your Lover lifts your bridal veil and says you are perfect in every way.

Remember Ivy Walker, the compelling young character in the movie *The Village*? She was blind but set out alone through an unfamiliar forest to obtain medicine needed by her dying fiancé. This brave and persistent young woman was led by love.

Like you and me, Ivy fought blindly to find her way through the wild and frightening forest, her hands stretched out into the darkness, feeling her way through the thicket of trees and brush and thistle. She was stumbling toward hope.

That's where you and I find ourselves when we fail to accept that in Jesus we are no longer blind, no longer lost, no longer burdened with guilt and shame. When we leave our smaller stories to enter God's Larger Story, we don't need to keep looking for home. God has found us, which means we are already home. We are safe in God's loving arms.

"Therefore, since we have such a hope, we are very bold," wrote Paul. "The veil is taken away."[5]

There is no more shame, no more guilt, no more ugliness. There is no more chasing after God, trying with all our might to catch him. There is not even any more stumbling toward hope.

In God's Larger Story we rest *in* hope. Resting in hope is about embracing the new covenant, accepting our new identities as God's own personal concern, leaving our smaller stories behind. Resting in hope is finally understanding the significance of God's furious pursuit.

Resting in hope means laying down the smaller story of human struggle and fully embracing the Larger Story of God's love.

LAY IT DOWN

"Therefore, since we are surrounded by so great a cloud of witnesses," wrote Paul, "let us also *lay aside every weight* and the sin that clings so closely…looking to Jesus the pioneer and perfecter of our faith."[6]

The story is no longer about us. It never was. As we live in God's Larger Story, we finally accept that he sees us, understands us, and loves us. Living fully in our new identity means that we fully embrace God's furious pursuit of us.

It is time to lay down the weight of our small, tired stories. We must lay down the weight of fear and shame and guilt, the weight of loneliness and rejection, the weight of feeling ugly and unaccepted and distant from God.

The words of Nichole Nordeman's tender ballad resonate with us all:

Everything I've carried on my own.
Lay it down, lay it down.[7]

Only when we lay down our feelings of worth-*less*-ness can we embrace our true identity. Only when we lay down the need to run *toward* hope, and instead begin resting *in* hope, will we feel accepted by God. Only when we leave behind our smaller stories can we grab hold of the love and forgiveness that God so freely extends.

Go ahead. Lay it down.

COME TO MOUNT ZION

Not so long ago I (Tim) was hiking a Colorado trail less than thirty minutes outside my hometown of Colorado Springs. It wound through some of the most breathtaking scenery on earth. The first leg of my hike was rather uneventful. I noticed a few squirrels and rabbits, a forest of trees, pits in the road, signs of erosion. It was nothing out of the ordinary. But the higher I hiked, the more the landscape changed. One bend in the trail fed into another; a false summit allowed glimpses of higher summits. Each new bend and each tantalizing view prodded me to keep climbing. I was hiking toward something grand and spectacular. I knew it was there even though I couldn't see it. My legs grew numb from fatigue, but I couldn't stop. I had to see where the trail led.

Finally, just when I thought my body could carry me no farther, I crested a hill to see a sight unlike anything I had ever seen. Creation exploded before me in a canvas of colors—colors I didn't know existed. In the far distance snowcapped mountains burst from the earth, stretching endlessly in all directions. Clouds billowed above them, clinging to the vast ocean of blue sky. A dozen shades of green swelled from the earth, rising and falling, embracing the curves of the hills and valleys. The air was crisp and clean and ripe with nature's perfume.

This was beauty that words can never fully capture.

I'm convinced it was a place just like this that inspired historian Thomas Berry when he described the "wisdom of nature:"

> The dawn and sunset are moments when the numinous source of all existence is experienced with special sensitivity. In springtime the flowering world sets forth its blossoms. The birds appear in the brilliance of their coloring, in the ease and skill of their flight, and in the beauty of their song.... Living things come into being, flourish, then fade from the scene. This ever-renewing sequence of sunrise and sunset, of seasonal succession, constitutes a pattern of life, a great liturgy, a celebration of existence.[8]

I saw what Berry had seen—"a celebration of existence." An endless festival of nature, far more than I could possibly take in. This was a sacred place, a place of glory and perfection. It was a place that perfectly illustrates where God wants you and me to reside.

"You have not come to a mountain that can be touched and that is burning with fire; to darkness, gloom and storm.... You have come to Mount Zion, to the heavenly Jerusalem, the city of the living God.... You have come to God...to Jesus the mediator of a new covenant."[9]

"You are the beautiful product of an extreme makeover," he is telling us, "a makeover of the spiritual kind. A covenant that is sealed for all time."

And this new covenant is for everyone. His grace is for everyone to share. Because of the passion of a God who will not be denied in his pursuit of us, our hope is no longer future, distant, or out of reach. Our hope is a fulfilled hope in which you and I now rest.

No Longer Running

Hope calls out, "Lay it down!" to everyone who lives in fear and guilt and shame. Hope cries out, "Lay it down!" to all who struggle with pain and resentment and anger. Hope embraces wounded hearts that have been scarred by loneliness and rejection. "Lay it down!" says hope.

Hope reaches out to every person who ever felt unworthy, every person who has longed to be understood by God. Hope calls to every Gomer who has prostituted herself, to every wayward son who has traveled to far-away lands to live with pigs, to every person who ever struggled with shame and doubt and remorse. Hope says, "Lay it down!"

Lay down whatever it is that keeps you from believing that the *furious pursuit* of God has caught you up into a mountaintop celebration of unspeakable grandeur, to the place where heaven and earth meet in a symphony beyond compare! To a place we no longer run *toward* but rest *in.*

Rest in the place where the veil is lifted and you are revealed to be everything you ever hoped you could be. Special. Desirable. Perfect in the eyes of God.

For all of us who once spent a lifetime *running toward hope,* now we *rest in hope*—today and forevermore.

NOTES

Acknowledgments

1. Psalm 115:1, NRSV.

Chapter 1

1. Psalm 88:14.
2. The description of the *Ziggy* cartoon as well as the wording on the map was taken from memory and may not duplicate the exact wording of the original. *Ziggy* is copyrighted and syndicated by Universal Press.
3. James 4:8.
4. Psalm 42:7, 9.
5. *The Village,* directed and produced by M. Night Shyamalan (Burbank, CA: Touchstone/Disney, 2004).
6. *The Village,* Touchstone/Disney.

Part I

1. The concept of God's pursuit of us is explored and developed throughout Scripture. The Exodus story screams of God's active intervention in our lives in his effort to pursue our hearts. Job struggled to understand why God allowed such turmoil to overcome him, and in the end we learn that it was all part of God's divine plan to teach Job (and us) a critical lesson. And everything Jonah experienced can be traced to God's pursuit of the prophet's heart. Everything that happens has meaning in God's economy.

2. See 2 Timothy 2:13.

3. See Romans 5:8.

Chapter 2

1. James Emery White, *Embracing the Mysterious God: Loving the God We Don't Understand* (Downers Grove, IL: InterVarsity, 2003), 9–10.

2. Sören Kierkegaard, "Philosophical Fragments," in *A Kierkegaard Anthology,* ed. Robert Bretall (Princeton, NJ: Princeton University Press, 1946), 165–66.

3. *Jerry Maguire,* written, directed, and produced by Cameron Crowe (Culver City, CA: Gracie Films/TriStar Pictures, 1996).

Chapter 3

1. 1 Corinthians 2:2.

2. Romans 8:1.

3. Brennan Manning, *Abba's Child: The Cry of the Heart for Intimate Belonging* (Colorado Springs: NavPress, 1994), 20.

4. Manning, *Abba's Child,* 21.

5. Louie Anderson, *Dear Dad: Letters from an Adult Child* (New York: Penguin, 1989), 16.

6. Anderson, *Dear Dad,* 20.

7. James Emery White, *Embracing the Mysterious God: Loving the God We Don't Understand* (Downers Grove, IL: InterVarsity, 2003), 21–22.

8. Psalm 77:1–3.

9. Dan Allender and Tremper Longman III, *The Cry of the Soul: How Our Emotions Reveal Our Deepest Questions About God* (Colorado Springs: NavPress, 1994), 30.

10. Bruce Nygren, *Touching the Shadows: A Love Tested and Renewed* (Nashville: Thomas Nelson, 2000), 50.

11. Psalm 77:6–9.

12. See Genesis 15:12–21.

13. Hebrews 6:13.

Chapter 4

1. Natalie Goldberg, *Writing Down the Bones: Freeing the Writer Within* (Boston: Shambhala, 1986), 16.

2. Goldberg, *Writing Down the Bones,* 16.

3. Brennan Manning, *The Ragamuffin Gospel: Embracing the Unconditional Love of God* (Portland: Multnomah, 1990), 38.

4. Will D. Campbell, *Brother to a Dragonfly* (New York: Continuum, 1987), 220, quoted in James Emery White, *Embracing the Mysterious God* (Downers Grove, IL: InterVarsity, 2003), 45.

5. Psalm 139:1–2, NASB.

6. Jack London, *The Call of the Wild, White Fang, and To Build a Fire* (New York: Random House, 1998), 258.

7. See Psalm 103:10–12, 14; 139:1–2, 13; Isaiah 43:25; John 8:1–11; Romans 5:8; 2 Timothy 2:13.

Chapter 5

1. See Ernest Hemingway, *The Sun Also Rises* (New York: Simon & Schuster, 1996).

2. See William Van Dusen Wishard, *Between Two Ages: The 21st Century and the Crisis of Meaning* (Boston: Shambhala, 2000), 103.

3. See Van Dusen Wishard, *Between Two Ages,* 103.

4. Iris Krasnow, *Surrendering to Marriage: Husbands, Wives, and Other Imperfections* (New York: Hyperion, 2001), 161.

5. Brennan Manning, *The Ragamuffin Gospel: Embracing the Unconditional Love of God* (Portland: Multnomah, 1990), 27–28.

6. See Romans 7:14–25.

7. *Dead Poets Society,* directed by Peter Weir (Burbank, CA: Silver Screen Partners IV/Touchstone Pictures, 1989).

8. Philippians 3:8–9.

9. According to one Greek-English lexicon, a more accurate translation from the original Greek would read "Consider everything dung...." For reference, see *A Greek-English Lexicon of the New Testament and Other Early Christian Literature,* eds. F. Wilbur Gingrich and Frederick W. Danker, 2nd ed. (Chicago: University of Chicago Press, 1979), 758.

10. In contrast to Old Testament demands, Paul saw God's Law as good and holy (see Romans 7:12). He also saw his hope in Christ taught in the Old Testament (see Acts 26:22) and pointed out that Gentiles come into the spiritual blessings of Israel (see Romans 15:27).

11. This is an allusion to Jack London's assessment of the foolish young prospector in his story "To Build a Fire." See Jack London, *The Call of the Wild, White Fang, and To Build a Fire* (New York: Random House, 1998), 258, emphasis added.

Part II

1. Matt Ridley, *Nature via Nurture: Genes, Experience, and What Makes Us Human* (New York: HarperCollins, 2003), 3–4.

Chapter 6

1. *The Dialogues of Plato: The Seventh Letter,* trans. Benjamin Jowett and J. Harward (Chicago: Encyclopaedia Britannica, 1952), 116.

2. See Genesis 1:26–27.

3. 2 Peter 1:4.

4. Claus Westermann, *Genesis 1–11: A Commentary,* trans. John J. Scullion S.J. (Minneapolis: Augsburg, 1984), 155–57, emphasis added.

5. Molly Marshall, *What It Means to Be Human* (Macon, GA: Smyth and Helwys, 1995), 19.

6. See 2 Peter 1:4.

7. See Psalm 103:10–12, 14; Romans 5:8.

8. Marshall, *What It Means,* 64, emphasis added.

9. Luke 15:18–19, NASB.

10. To read the complete story, see Luke 15:11–32.

Chapter 7

1. See Ezekiel 16:53.

2. For further study on Israel's schools for prophets, see 1 Samuel 10:5, 10 (Gibeah); 1 Samuel 19:19–20 (Ramah); 2 Kings 2:3 (Bethel); 2 Kings 2:5 (Jericho); 2 Kings 4:38 (Gilgal).

3. Hosea 1:2, author's paraphrase.

4. Hosea 1:2.

5. Hosea 2:7, NLT.

6. James 4:17, author's paraphrase.

7. Hosea 2:14–15.

8. Hosea 2:15.

9. Psalm 139:7–10.

Chapter 8

1. Although Western society is preoccupied with linear time, that doesn't mean our Hebrew ancestors did not view history as linear as well—as moving into the promises of God.

2. Luke 12:24.

3. See Genesis 32:22–32.

4. Proverbs 13:12.

5. Henry David Thoreau, *Walden and Other Writings* (New York: Random House, 1992), 7.

Chapter 9

1. Ezekiel 16:4–8, HCSB.

2. Ezekiel 16:8, HCSB.

3. Dylan Thomas, "Fern Hill," in *The Poems of Dylan Thomas* (New York: New Directions, 2003), 195. *The Poems of Dylan Thomas,* copyright © 1945 by The Trustees for the Copyrights of Dylan Thomas. Reprinted by permission of New Directions Publishing Corp.

4. Frederick Buechner, *The Sacred Journey: A Memoir of Early Days* (New York: HarperCollins, 1982), 39.

5. David Crowder, *Praise Habit: Finding God in Sunsets and Sushi* (Colorado Springs: NavPress, Th1nk, 2004), 11.

6. Psalm 139:16, NRSV.

7. Romans 8:28, NASB.

8. Luke 7:47, NRSV.

9. For further study on this passage, see Paul Tillich, *The New Being* (New York: Scribner, 1955), 7.

10. Isaiah 44:22, NRSV.

11. 1 John 4:19.

Part III

1. William Barclay, *The Mind of Jesus* (New York: Harper & Row, 1976), 3.

Chapter 10

1. See *The International Standard Bible Encyclopedia,* ed. Geoffrey W. Bromiley, vol. 1 (Grand Rapids: Eerdmans, 1979), 608.

2. See 1 Corinthians 1:27.

3. Song of Songs 1:15.

4. Song of Songs 2:2.

5. Song of Songs 2:14.

6. Song of Songs 4:7, 9, NRSV.

7. John 13:1.

8. John 13:4–5.

9. 1 John 4:19.

10. John 13:8.

11. John Betjeman, "In a Bath Teashop," public domain.

Chapter 11

1. Romans 6:4; Colossians 2:12, NLT.

2. Mark 15:34.

3. Psalm 22:1, 7–8, 16, 18.

4. Psalm 22:24.

5. Psalm 22:30–31.

6. See Hebrews 5:7.

7. Joshua 1:5.

Chapter 12

1. See Matthew 7:24–27.

2. T. Britten and G. Lyle, "What's Love Got to Do with It," copyright © 1993, Virgin Records.

3. Romans 8:38–39.

4. Nichole Nordeman, "Hold On," copyright © 2005, EMI Music.

5. The Tramp, "Jesus' Blood Never Failed Me Yet," public domain. As the story implies, the song has no known origin other than these simple lyrics sung by a homeless man outside a London train station. The song was set to music by Gavin Bryars and first performed in December 1972 at Queen Elizabeth Hall. It was later released on the soundtrack "Jesus' Blood Never Failed Me Yet," conducted by Michael Riesman, composed by Gavin Bryars, and performed by Tom Waits. The soundtrack was released by Phillips Studios in August 1993. For more on the story of this song, see *www.gavin bryars.com.*

Chapter 13

1. 2 Corinthians 3:18.

2. See Genesis 15:12–21.

3. Hebrews 6:13.

4. 2 Corinthians 3:9–11, NKJV.

5. 2 Corinthians 3:12, 16.

6. Hebrews 12:1–2, NRSV.

7. Nichole Nordeman, "Lay It Down," copyright © 2005, EMI Music.

8. Thomas Berry, *The Great Work: Our Way into the Future* (New York: Bell Tower, 1999), 177.

9. Hebrews 12:18, 22–24.

CONTINUE TO EMBRACE
THE CHASE

For additional resources, visit

WWW.FURIOUSPURSUIT.COM

- FREE sermon outlines for pastors

- Audio CD to accompany the workbook study

- Download a facilitator's guide for conducting small groups